PREFACE TO 2006 EDITION

For 22 years, now, readers have been using this book to negotiate wonderful salary packages.

A special thanks to the many many people who have taken a moment to call me or email me their success stories. I always appreciate hearing them.

Here's some version. 2006 highlights:

• **Telecoaching.** Readers have been so enthusiastic about the results they got from my salary-telecoaching service that I have included some examples in Chapter 12. [You're invited to enlist me personally as a coach in this regard, too. Check out chapter 12.]

• **Internet Salary Research** section is expanded, offering you several websites with reviews.

• When to **get it in writing** is expanded.

• **Negotiating by Email.** Readers asked how to handle salary communication by email—my thoughts in Chapter 8.

• **Achieving Financial Independence.** At the end of Chapter 12, you'll find information about a free report on three ways to get out of the salary negotiating syndrome altogether by achieving financial freedom without changing careers.

This edition is supplemented with articles you'll find on my website www.SalaryNegotiations.com. You'll also find updates on internet resources and other goodies. The password for some of that web-based information is BoughtTheBook.

AUG 2008

NEGOTIATING YOUR SALARY:

HOW TO MAKE $1,000 A MINUTE

by JACK CHAPMAN

Jack welcomes comments and questions about this book or career-consulting work.

Quantity Order Discount: for information about discounts on orders of 25 or more copies of this book, contact the author directly. 847-251-4727

Contact information:

Address: Jack Chapman, 511 Maple Ave., Wilmette, IL 60091

Voice: (847) 251-4727.

Fax: 847-256-4690

E-mail: jkchapman@aol.com

Website: http://www.SalaryNegotiations.com

© 1987, 1992 by Ten Speed Press.

© 1996, Third Edition, by Jack Chapman.

© 2000, Fourth Edition, by Jack Chapman

© 2006, Fifth Edition, by Jack Chapman

Printed in the United States of America

Illustrations by Karen Barrie

C.I.P. data on file with publisher

ISBN: 978-1-58008-776-6

DEDICATION

To all the clients I have worked with over the years; I learned my craft by helping you achieve your own career satisfaction and success.

CONTENTS

ACKNOWLEDGEMENTS

Special thanks for helping me create this book go to:

Janet Butler, my faithful salary-business companion, who has goo gobs (one of her favorite words; you'll see it in Chapter 5) of faith in the power of this book to make money for its readers and has kept my shoulder to the wheel in salary-coaching endeavors. She genuinely enjoys seeing people prosper.

Mary-Ellen Mort, M.L.S., who helped me understand the intricacies of getting online salary information.

Marti Beddoe and Robin Sheerer, who have been this career consultant's career consultants and cheering section.

Chuck Sterbis, my colleague in career consulting, who offered strategic criticism about the methods presented here.

Dan Felix, "The Executive's Attorney," who penned some good advice about when to use a lawyer.

Anne Troy, whose technical editing vastly improved the readability. She took me to places in Microsoft Word few tourists ever see.

And most important, Karen, my wife, whose vision encouraged me to go for it, and whose practical love and support made it possible.

Chapter 1
Million-Dollar Blunders

Calculating the Dollars You Can Make, or Lose, in Those Sixty Seconds of Negotiations

We spend years thinking about what we'll be when we grow up. We put thousands of dollars and hours into school to get a degree and then spend weeks on résumés, letters, and ads. We schlep from city to suburb to city, talking to jerks, jokes, and gentlemen about their job openings. We put hours of practice into a sales pitch, hours of research into understanding the company, and two or three nervous days into interviews, straining to beat out the competition. The most important part, the whole reason we started in the first place—**getting paid**—we often handle in sixty seconds or less!

For months afterwards, we roll up our sleeves and give our new job every ounce of brains and drive we can supply. But when it's time for a raise, most of us just accept whatever we're offered. How many minutes do we spend negotiating the money? *Zero.*

However, sixty seconds is all you'll need to negotiate either a salary or a raise. You'll learn in this book how to make those sixty seconds count. You'll learn how to make thousands of dollars in that minute, and how to improve your whole sense of work and worth.

Consider for a moment how that adds up.

A modest-to-low annual lifetime wage, beginning at, say, $15,000 a year and ending at $60,000, averages out to be $30,000 a year. Over forty-five years, that totals $1,125,000! So even a simple 10-percent original raise that provides a larger base for all subsequent raises means an extra $1,350,00 over that time. You could buy your home with just a 10-percent raise!

That's just the start. Proper negotiations can *double* your income. Mishandling negotiations can be a million-dollar blunder.

And it's easy to blunder. In my many years as a personal career- and salary-coach, I've seen people earning only half their value just because they never correctly asked for more. How would you handle these three situations?

Million-Dollar Blunders

Example 1: Mr. Eager Loses the Offer

Mr. Eager is bright, ambitious, and interested in working hard. He expects to be paid fairly and at the top of his range. His potential employer is looking at Eager's record. The résumé looks good and Eager has just the kind of experience the company could use and some solid examples of making things work right.

Desirous not to waste his time, Eager pops the question in the most tactful way he can. "Well, let's see if we're in the right ball park. I'm looking for a salary in the middle sixties."

Mr. Employer figures the amount is okay, but is just a touch put off. He thinks Eager should primarily be interested in long-term work with the company. Eager's approach makes it sound as if he's more interested in the money. Well, that's understandable, but Mr. Employer is also interviewing Mr. Dedicated for the job. Although he doesn't know what

Dedicated's price range is, it certainly sounds as if *he's* interested in the company. "After all," Mr. Employer decides, "I built this company from the ground up in the last ten years. I want team players."

"Well," Mr. Employer tells Eager, "we might be able to meet that; let's keep talking."

Sounds promising but, when all is said and done, Mr. Employer picks Dedicated. "I want a company man," Mr. Employer reasons, "and I'm willing to go to the middle sixties to get him. After all, Dedicated must be worth at least as much as Eager." Eager loses the offer.

Example 2: Ms. Polite Loses $7,500 a Year

Ms. Polite knows that women make just over seventy-nine cents to a man's dollar. She has corporate aspirations, though, and a solid background to build them on. Now that an M.B.A. has been added to the top of her résumé, she's got the technical education to back up her ambitions. But the job market is tough and competition amounts to survival of the fittest.

"We're budgeted at $67,500 for this position, Polite," says Mr. S. Tablishment, "and we really shouldn't talk any further unless that figure fits your requirements."

"Hmm," Polite thinks, "not quite what I expected, but no use quibbling now; I want to stay in the running. I can't reject it. Better give in here and negotiate later."

"That seems fair," she says. "Tell me more about the qualities you're looking for."

Thursday, Polite's phone rings. "Mr. Tablishment calling." He says his firm is offering her the job, but she should decide right away because he has to contact the other candidates.

"Oh my," she thinks, "if I push now, I might lose the offer. Better say yes and negotiate a raise later based on my performance."

On Friday Tablishment tells his comptroller, "Harry, I know we had $75,000 set aside for the new position, but you can put $7,500 of that into my travel-and-entertainment budget. I've found someone with real potential, and she'll start at $67,500."

So Polite loses an annual $7,500, *and all the raises based on that.*

Example 3: Mr. Hardwork Loses His Raise

Mr. Hardwork is hoping for a substantial raise this year. His accounts have perfect records and 10-percent-better profits than last year. Several customers have written to the company to say what a conscientious job he's doing.

The raise is a week overdue, actually, because his boss has been discussing raises and overall compensation with the board since January. The grapevine has rumored that the raises will surface on Groundhog Day.

On February 9, Hardwork finds a note in his mailbox praising him for all his fine work the past year and acknowledging his wonderful contributions. It also informs him that he has been awarded a "very generous" 5-percent raise.

Hardwork feels cheated. Complaining bitterly of how unfair that is, he storms into his boss's office saying he deserves at least 10 percent for his outstanding work.

"Gosh," says the boss, "we've really gone over all the records thoroughly. The board personnel have looked at them and consulted industry standards. That's the best we can do. But tell you what, I'll talk one on one with the CEO and mention you specifically, and we'll see what we can do."

Hardwork never got that extra 5 percent, and he didn't think to make it up by negotiating perks like vacation time, education, car, health-club membership, bonuses, and IRA contributions.

Hardwork lost half his raise. Don't let that happen to you.

The Principle of Quality

Winning at salary and raise negotiations requires, first of all, understanding the principle of quality.

"Quality is remembered long after price is forgotten," I was told by an accomplished salesman who was a client of mine. He reminded me that the many "bargains" I'd picked up in my life had worn out quickly, broken, or performed only after silent prayers or loud curses. I then remembered the times when I'd paid dearly for the "top of the line." Almost every one of those tools, appliances, and articles of clothing is still with me. Each time I use or wear one of them I relish the craftsmanship and care, admire the fit and effectiveness, and appreciate the durability.

Compensation negotiating is about those kinds of purchases. It is about the joy and satisfaction you will bring to employers when they see their investment in quality—*yours*—compounded daily, easing their minds, and making more money for their businesses.

Smart employers know there's no free lunch where talent is concerned. The relentless downsizing of the 80s and 90s has produced "lean and mean" companies where every single person's contribution counts. The proliferation of popular management books extolling the team-oriented approach to profitability also brings home the truth that human resources are the most valuable elements in a successful enterprise. On one hand, employers understand that they have to pay quality prices for quality personnel. On the other hand, since they are successful business people, they try to get the best quality for the lowest price.

Their job is to make good business deals. *Your* job is to see that they recognize your quality and pay you your best price. If you don't, it can cost you thousands of dollars and a big chunk of your self-esteem.

Let me show you how much better your working life can be when you do it the right way.

The Difference between Vicious and Virtuous Cycles

First consider the vicious cycle. Mr. Drone is overworked, underpaid, and undervalued. His attitude is less than 100-percent enthusiastic and his work of course shows it. His co-workers notice it, too, and the boss is secretly glad she didn't give that extra 10 percent because, after all, Drone is performing only adequately.

"Raise?" she says. "Clean up these performance reviews and we'll consider it."

Maybe Drone says, "I quit!"

Perhaps the boss retorts, "You're fired!"

Or maybe Drone just quietly shuts down. He does his job absent-mindedly, waiting for the moment when he, Walter Mitty-like, can walk out on the place on the busiest day of the year. "Then they'll miss me," he says. "They'll be sorry!"

Sooner or later, one way or another, Drone is out the door. To be polite, his employer gives him an innocuous letter of recommendation damning him with faint praise. Drone and his ego, a little worse for wear, hit the job market wondering, "Am I really worth that extra 10 percent?"

He sheepishly exaggerates when interviewers ask, "What was your last salary?" And since they weren't born yesterday, they pick up that Drone either didn't make that much or isn't convinced he was worth it.

A few desperate weeks pass. Drone's ego, once tall, is now barely crawling into interviews. Finally, someone offers him a job! Not quite what he expected, but it beats unemployment, and maybe *this* employer will notice his value and give him more money later.

The vicious cycle begins again, a little more entrenched.

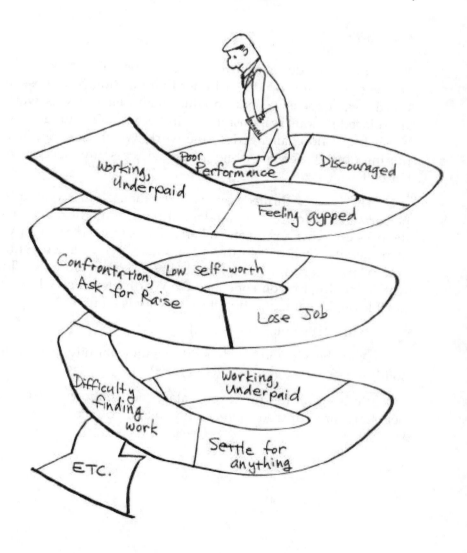

Figure 1-1. Entrenched in the Vicious Cycle

Ms. Worth

Now consider the virtuous cycle, the story of Ms. Worth. She negotiated for top dollar in her first position. Her boss knew Worth was expensive, but convinced himself she was worth it, and placed serious responsibilities in her job. Encouraged by her boss's trust and challenged by the work, Worth extended herself, putting out 120 percent while tucking success after success under her belt.

The boss is thrilled, but worries that, after a year of such performance, Worth, such a talented person, might move on. So the boss gives her a raise and a hefty bonus to keep her happy, but to no avail. One of Worth's co-workers is impressed with her quality and praises her to a friend, who is connected to Mr. Jones, who is looking for someone just like Worth. Jones is willing to be flexible on the compensation if the quality is there.

"Sure, let's talk," says Worth.

And the virtuous cycle starts again—happily, a little more solidified.

Both scenarios hinge on salary negotiations. When you negotiate for your true value, both you and your company win.

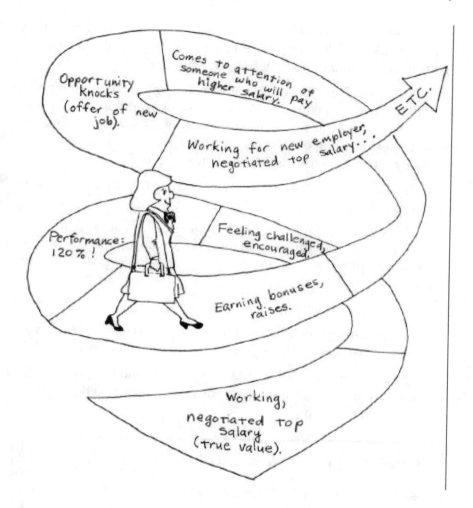

Figure 1-2. The virtuous cycle of Ms. Worth.

Here's what's ahead.

The next chapter gives you the basic principle of effective salary negotiations and, hopefully, instills in you more confidence to venture into negotiations.

Then Chapters Three through Seven lay out The Five Salary Making rules. Following those rules assures your best chance of getting every dollar and benefit possible.

Chapter Eight and Nine cover the most frequent special situations you'll encounter, including stock options. For people who've acquired this book, my website www.SalaryNegotiations.com has articles covering even more special situations. You can access those by using the password BoughtTheBook.

Then comes raises in Chapter Ten! You'll learn how to maximize those.

Finally: coaching! The last chapter shows you how to reach me so my coaching can personally guide you to apply what you learn here. [It's not complicated, just dial 847-853-1046.] It pays for itself.

On to the principle!

Negotiating well is simply following five rules. "Five?" you say, "That's all?" Yes—you can remember 5 rules, right?

Here are the five Salary Making Rules ahead of you. You'll get to know and understand each one as you progress through chapters two through six.

Salary-Making Rule 1: When to Discuss Money.

Salary-Making Rule 2: Who Goes First.

Salary Making Rule 3: Your First Response

Salary Making Rule 4: Your Researched Response

Salary Making Rule 5: Clinch the Deal and Deal Some More.

Figure 1-2. Preview of Things to Come

Chapter 2
Aiming for What You're Worth

Good negotiations, like Ms. Worth's, are ones in which both sides applaud the outcome. Employees like Worth feel appreciated and motivated, and their bosses feel they've hired someone of quality who's worth every penny. Obviously, it pays to follow Worth's example and go for top dollar.

But how do you know what top dollar is? How will you know what's too little? Is it possible to reach too high? How can you tell what you are really worth?

Later I'll show you how to zero in on your objective market-value using internet resources (in Chapter Five); that's one measure of what you are worth. For now, though, let's explore beyond the objective market-value measure and ask, even more fundamentally, how you can tell what you are really worth.

To find out, we need to look at the situation through employers' eyes and bring up the three principles employers have in mind when budgeting a salary or raise.

First Principle: Labor Is Intangible

Salespeople can tell you there are two kinds of products: tangibles and intangibles. Employers consider that a person's labor is among the latter. Note the contrast: While the price of a tangible is easily determined by applying the formula:

$$\text{Raw Materials} + \text{Production Costs} + 10\% \text{ Profit} = \text{Price,}$$

For intangibles there are no raw materials or production costs and the first two variables in that equation equal zero.

So the employer's first principle is *Labor is intangible.* An employer buys your labor. But your labor is even less like a tangible TV or car because, after the deal for it is struck, your labor can fall short of expectations, or constantly improve, since it is entirely under human control—yours. The more you can do, the more complicated are the problems you can solve for someone, and the more your labor should be worth. Measuring that worth can be a full-time job. It's called compensation analysis.

But employers know that, even when a compensation analyst has set a figure for a particular job, it's only an educated guess, a guideline. Some workers are worth several thousand more because they do that much more, while others accomplish less and therefore deserve smaller checks.

Since labor is an intangible, employers know there's no fixed price, no number chiseled in granite; rather, there is a range.

Second Principle: Salary Relates to Level of Responsibility

The employer's second principle is *The main variable that determines compensation is the extent of the employee's responsibilities.* The more people or products an employee's decisions affect, the more money those decisions influence as well. Salary is merely an indicator of that responsibility.

The typists in a law firm, for instance, have little effect on business. Others decide what they will type, and still others check their work. The paralegal's research, however, actually helps win a case. And the associate attorney's contribution is crucial to getting the case resolved. But it is the experience, courtroom savvy, and legal thinking of the partners who consult with and direct the associates that ultimately pay all their salaries. If they win the case, everyone will share the glory; if they lose, the partners will take the blame. The partners shoulder the most responsibility, so they make the most money.

A classic example from the seventies: Lee Iacocca's decisions won or lost millions of dollars for struggling Chrysler corporation in an instant, and his salary reflected that colossal responsibility. Experienced securities analysts, too, earn six figures, but only because their decisions make seven or eight figures for the portfolios they direct.

The [Third, and] Universal Hiring Principle Is *Make Me a Buck*

The employer's third principle is very simple. The "universal hiring principle," as careers author Tom Jackson terms it, is *Make me a buck.*

This principle seems to say that, if you show employers you'll make them even a dollar more than you cost, they should hire you. In actual practice, however, when you add up telephones, desk space, support staff, equipment, hiring costs, training costs, medical benefits, FICA, standard perks, vacations, and other expenses, *your decisions and labor must gross a company several times your salary to make hiring you worthwhile.*

I've often had clients tell me, "Oh, I don't know if I could ever take one of those commission jobs. I need a secure income."

Hey, I've got news for them! We *all* work on commission. We all earn only a percentage of what we make for the company. Take a look at 1982 and 1991 and post 911, when recessions hit everyone's sales. Who lost their jobs? Commissioned salespeople? No, they just worked harder. It was the middle management, support staff, and CEOs who were no longer cost effective and got their pink slips.

Either you make more for your employer than you cost, or you go. Even charitable, nonprofit agencies pay on a type of "commission." Either their employees contribute work that other people believe in and "pay" for with charitable donations or they, too, become nonprofit.

Would you believe it's true in government, too? Government is more nearly immune to the profit principle because it's supposed to provide public services, not make a profit and if it runs out of money, it can just levy and collect more taxes. How does *Make me a buck* apply there?

Elected officials' salaries depend on the support of the voters. They will continue to get paid only if they are reelected, which is their reward for delivering or promising services that the people appreciate. To deliver those goodies from the public coffers, however, government must either more or less balance the budget or raise taxes. And raising taxes can be the easiest way for politicians to fire themselves. If an official pushes for something the voters notice and don't like, poof! He or she is gone.

So the political *Make me a buck* is more accurately expressed as Make me a vote to make me a buck. Unless an employee is doing work that is cost effective, within the budget, and likely to get the boss reelected, bye-bye!

When it comes to putting an actual dollar figure on a government employee's contribution, the federal government and most other governmental units have very rigid step and grade systems for compensating their bureaucrats. Since public-service employees do not produce money but merely transfer it from one citizen to another, there's no profitability to determine for them. So government typically looks to the profit-making sector, compares duties, chooses a salary, and locks it in. Therefore, even those in the nonprofit sector get paid by the *Make me a buck* profit-making principle.

Example 4 illustrates the employer's need for employees to generate more money than they cost.

Million-Dollar Blunders

Example 4: Mr. Greedy Gets What He Deserves

Mr. Greedy has a technical and managerial decision-making background he thinks is worth $65,000 a year. His education supports that assessment, too. But he clearly has the potential to handle work worth $125,000 or more in the long run, and he was hard at work on his job search.

He approached a high-tech manufacturing firm to explore a very competitive position. After a thorough discussion, the head honcho said, "You aren't qualified for the big-buck positions yet, but I think you have potential." He further hinted that, if Greedy was willing to come aboard at a lower level and get some exposure and experience, perhaps he would gain a competitive edge for future openings. "Of course," the president misguessed, "this lower-level production position would not pay you what you're worth, because we could do only $80,000 to $90,000 on it, but you could consider it."

Greedy, of course, was ecstatic. The position paid $15,000 over his fondest hopes, for work that seemed very doable. Instead of being cautious at being overpaid, he let it stand that the seventies was the range for him.

Greedy's further interviews with the firm's senior managers left them less convinced of his long-term potential than the president had been.

Why, they reasoned, should we hand over $90,000 for a $65,000 production job when we don't know if this guy will really work out in the long term? They might have been willing to pay him $55,000 to $60,000 and judge his performance over time. However, the president had boxed the company in by committing to at least $80,000, and Greedy had boxed himself in by agreeing too soon to be overpaid. So instead they sent Greedy a TNT (Thanks, no thanks) letter saying, "We do not see a match between your career goals and our firm at this time."

Greedy, saying that he'd consider anything to get into that field, tried, of course, to defuse the salary issue, but it was hard to do without sounding desperate. These people had no time to review the five-person decision further. So it goes.

Greedy should have defused the salary question right away instead of operating on a get-all-I-can principle. A quick comment to keep the potential job alive might have gone like this: "Well, it's really too early to discuss salary. I just want a fair salary for whatever responsibilities I handle. Let's first discuss how I can help you."

Effective Salary Negotiations

The best outcome in salary negotiations, then, is based on these three principles.

- Labor is an intangible
- Salary relates to level of responsibility
- Employees must make more money for the company than they cost.

We've also noted that being greedy can boomerang. The answer to the question "How much am I really worth?" is "Only what's fair and competitive for the quantity and quality of work you contribute." And since your contributions can be greater or less than another person's in that "same" job, what's fair and competitive is not a fixed price, but a range. You should aim for the top of that range.

How do we define the best outcome? When you examine your present compensation or look at a new salary, and you can say "I'm paid the very best my skills can get in this company in this market." you will have made an excellent bargain.

That's the basic principle of effective salary negotiations. It helps insure that both sides will be happy. Good negotiations, after all, are always win-win negotiations.

In Chapter 5 you'll learn a formula and method to research your market value so you'll know exactly what range to request for a specific position. We'll discuss all current e-resources and others, for researching your range. Now, however, you're about to shake hands with Mr. Employer and step into his office.

Chapter 3
Salary-Making Rule 1:
When to Discuss Money

Mr. Employer walks into the waiting room and introduces himself. You smile and shake hands. He leads you to his office, invites you to sit down, and then describes the job he's interviewing you for. Next he glances at your résumé and poses a few questions about your qualifications. You do your best to convince him of your quality. Now Mr. Employer looks you straight in the eye and asks, "By the way, what sort of a salary are you looking for?"

What do you do?

Follow Salary-Making Rule 1, which instructs that one time and one time only is appropriate for talking salary. In a moment, I'll tell you exactly when that is. For now, here's a hint: This is not it.

To understand why that's so, you first need to learn an odd yet true piece of human nature that applies to all of us, including Mr. Employer.

Ever Bought Something You Couldn't Afford?

One question I always ask in my seminars is, "Have you ever bought something you couldn't afford?"

All in the audience pause, look blank for a moment, then break into nods and smiles while remembering the things that they "couldn't afford" while buying. They pause because the left side of the brain, the logical side, knows it's a contradiction in terms; you can't buy something you can't afford. If you do, it means that you really *can* afford it. But the right side of the brain, the visionary side, remembers the painful struggle, the exciting resolution, and the pleasure that had been gained from unaffordable purchases.

Do you own a house? Could you afford it when you bought it? Do you own a car? Could you afford *it* when you bought it? Think of anything really expensive that you've bought: a special vacation, for example. Before you decided to spend the money, did you think of yourself as someone who could afford that kind of thing?

How do people get to the point of buying something they can't afford? Usually they progress from being curious to interested, intrigued, then wanting it, wanting it a lot, wondering how they can get it, thinking about it almost all the time, scheming, scrimping, saving, and finally buying it because they just can't *stand* not having it any more! Then they wonder how they ever get along without it.

My term for this process is *budget bending*. During this process, as the urge to buy grows stronger, people make their money supply grow, too, by making it more flexible. We can divide its progressive flexibility into three stages that I call **budget**, **fudgit**, and **judgit**.

The first stage is familiar to everybody. No matter at what point a new desire creeps in, it's met with money's first line of defense, the **budget**.

Figure 3-1. An in-creeping spending urge is met by money's first line of defense: The Budget.

*A **budget** is the way we hold on to the illusion that we are controlling our finances.* In handling money, we all like to feel in charge. The easiest way to do that is to count how many dollars come in, divide them into little piles, and name one pile "rent," another "food," another "savings," and so on. So at the end of the month, we've parceled out the income and transformed it into outgo and we're at zero again. We feel in control.

Now, that's not really controlling our finances.   It's like adding water to the soup until it's thin enough to give everybody a cupful or like "steering" a canoe down rapids.

But it's very comfortable to live within a budget structure. Living within one allows us not to afford things we're scared of, cry "poor," complain about the economy, and lead a simple, organized existence at the same time.   That's **budget**, or living within our means, the most rigid stage.

Although we might yearn to own a Mercedes, our budget won't allow it; so we leave it until the day we win the lottery. But our next-door neighbor gets a Mercedes, and then *his* neighbor does. We find ourselves reading the Mercedes ads instead of the business section of *Time*.   Our desire erodes our budgetary concern and slips us into **fudgit**, the financial status quo's next defense.

In the **fudgit** stage we still think income is constant but are willing to shuffle the outgo to make room for new things.

"Maybe if I quit smoking, walk to work, buy my clothes on sale, and deduct the car's principal and interest as business expenses, I, too, could buy a Mercedes."   The key word there is "maybe."   Purchases are rarely made in the **fudgit** stage. Since money is still not flexible, budget juggling doesn't usually provide all the extra cash needed, but it gets us closer. Working through the **fudgit** stage gets us ready to take the plunge if the object goes on sale, or if we just can't stand it any more.

However, the sure way to get from maybe to yes is to go through the **judgit** stage.

Say one day we casually ask our neighbor with the Mercedes how he can afford it. "Well, I'm in real estate," he says, "so I shut down the office. Now I run my business out of my car; computer, fax, wireless internet, cell phone, files are all I the trunk; that way I save all that rent and other overhead." (That's **fudgit**.)

"But that doesn't really cover it. The most important part is that when my clients see me in my Mercedes office on wheels, they are really impressed. My sales have jumped because people take me seriously, and referral business has improved since I'm almost always there to answer the phone." (That's **judgit.**)

Figure 3-2. Shuffling the outgo of money to make room for new things: The Fudgit Stage.

Notice how the actual *quantity* of money available becomes flexible. The **judgit** stage takes an objective but creative look at the Mercedes and sees it not as a liability but as a money-making asset. Of course we can't afford it now, but the only way ever to afford it is to buy it! So in the light of long-term thinking, we can be most expansive and flexible about the money. The same thing happens when we decide to spend $5,000 on a new, efficient heating system we "can't afford." It will pay for itself over the next three to five years. We'll buy an item of superior quality now and save fuel and replacement costs later.

Waiting for the Right Moment

The best moment to talk salary with Mr. Employer is when he's reached the judgit stage. Let me show you why.

Employers are always curious about your most recent salary for just one reason: to screen you. When faced with a lot of applicants, they use salary as a quick, shorthand way of assessing the fit and narrowing down the list.

They don't want to waste interviewing time, so they screen out people they "can't afford." They also cross off people who are below their range. They can afford those people, but, since salary is related to degree of responsibility, employers think someone earning less than the budgeted range probably couldn't handle the job. Restricting interviews according to salary, therefore, is intended to get the most competent help for the least possible money. This is the employer's budget stage.

While screening for the least expensive capable candidate, however, the boss or personnel officer may scratch you off the list regardless of whether you could really do the work or are even the best person for the job. Even if you passed the screening, you'd be locked into the figure you quoted and would lose the opportunity to get the best market price for your skills.

Is it ever in your interest to be screened? If you're qualified for the job, no! Don't talk salary yet. Salary-Making Rule 1 is *Postpone salary discussions until you have been offered the job.*

Figure 3-3. In The Judgit Stage anything is possible, even a real-estate office on wheels!

When Mr. Employer offers you the job, he's either *in* the judgit stage, or as close to it as he's going to get. He's convinced you're the best candidate. Therefore, he's more willing to make the pay scale flexible, and even practice creative budget juggling, to get you.

The same applies to raises. There, the rule is "Wait to discuss a raise until after your performance review." (See Chapter 10, "Raises and Salary Reviews.") If your performance review has been impressive, your boss will be poised at the judgit stage, ready to be flexible about money. Since you've been convincing about your quality, your raise is a new salary—as if you're being rehired at a new rate.

There's another reason to postpone salary discussions until the job has been offered. Let's take an example from your own shopping experience.

If you want to buy a DVD player, you check out several stores. Suppose you get a price quotation from every salesperson except one, who says, "Look, here is what I have. I think it's the quality you want. So if I'm right, before you buy anywhere else come back and talk to me about price. I'm sure we can make a deal." Would you at least check in there before buying if you thought he would give you the best price? Of course. But if he had quoted $119, and in your fourth store you saw the equivalent for $125, would you bother to go back for $6.00? Probably not. Keeping a price flexible and open motivates people to check back before deciding.

So if you table salary negotiations until you have a nod from potential employers, they're likely at least to check back with you before their final round.

But what if the job doesn't pay in your range, anyway? Aren't you just wasting your time and theirs by interviewing? Yes. But what in the world are you doing interviewing for a job below your level of responsibility?

You'd better do some homework or hire a career consultant to get yourself focused on the right kinds of positions. You should be able to screen the job with respect to how much responsibility it requires. If the job challenges you comfortably, the right money should follow.

How to Postpone Salary Talk: Part I

By now you may be thinking, "Okay, it sounds like a good idea to put off discussing salary until I've been offered the job. But how do I do that? When Mr. Employer asks me right away what salary I'm looking for, I can't just ignore the question."

True. Here's what you can do. You can respond confidently to any premature salary gambit with the reply, "I'm sure we can come to a good salary agreement if I'm the right person for the job, so let's first agree on whether I am." Or: "Salary? Well, so far the job seems to have the right amount of responsibility for me, and I'm sure you pay a fair salary, don't you?" (What can he say?) "So let's hold off on salary talk until you know you want me. What other areas should we discuss now?"

Some of my other clients have answered the question "What are your salary requirements?" with "Are you offering me the job?"

Other handy phrases can be found at the end of the next chapter. There are many polite ways to postpone salary talk. These delays in discussing money can give you time to move your potential employer from budget to fudgit to judgit.

The Preemptive Strike

My acknowledgments to Marty Nemko, author of *Cool Careers for Dummies*, for the following technique which I've dubbed the Preemptive Strike. Marty suggests that instead of postponing salary talk, you, the candidate, should bring it up early and get it out of the way. I'm impressed: I think this can work!

We differ as to why you'd do it, but we agree it takes the pressure off. Marty suggests it, I believe, as a way around Salary-Making Rule 1. In his opinion, it's better to "do it up front and get it out of the way" than to postpone it. My perspective on Marty's method is that it's a marvelous way to actually follow Salary-Making Rule 1. If you find it awkward to play "dodge the salary" when the employer brings it up you can head off that entire scene using his "handle it now" technique.

[BTW I like his book; he "breaks the rules" of conventional career counseling and the thinking is refreshing. His book, actually, recommends you wait for "the moment when the boss seems maximally enthusiastic about ... you working for him," which in my interpretation means wait until there's an offer. It's in conversation with him that he proposed this alternative to postponing salary talk.]

Here's how the preemptive strike works. After you have developed some rapport with the interviewer and have had some discussion about your skills, the job, etc., you casually pop this question, "By the way, Mr. Employer, I know it's too early to discuss compensation in detail, but I wonder if you can give me a rough idea of the range you were thinking of with regard to this position?"

It doesn't matter much what they answer! Later, when you get to the judgit stage you'll still be able to negotiate your best price. What does matter is that by getting them to spill the beans, you avoid them asking you what your salary expectations are. On the other hand, this option runs a small risk of appearing more interested in money than the job and the risk, too, of them turning the tables and asking about your expectations.

And once they've answered? The following response will steer you back on the main road, "Thank you. I'm confident if I'm the right person for the job we can find a salary that works." Then focus attention back on the job interview with, "Tell me more about the key problems you want handled on this job," or, "Let's discuss the management style your company wants to see." Any question that puts the interviewer back on exploring the match between you and the job/company will do.

Notice how this question and reply not only helps the employer relax about being able to afford you, but also postpones real salary discussion until later. Properly done, your reply doesn't accept the range as-is, you're still free to negotiate more.

What if They Get Angry with Me?

Chapter 10 covers handling this worry in more detail, and when to disobey the rules in order to avoid tension and anger in the interview. Sometimes, going first can be the right thing to do, but that's higher learning; get proficient at the basics first. *So, definitely read Chapter 10 – but not yet.* For now, let's look at how we might avoid any struggle.

I must admit that it feels a little tense when an employer asks about your salary requirements and you won't disclose them.

A tug of war over disclosing your money requirements hurts your chances of being hired because it destroys the rapport needed for hiring. Your rule of thumb here is to put off the first request, maybe the second, but if asked again you'll need to handle it more directly.

Here are ways to handle it and avoid a struggle.

Soften your "Let's wait" statements with introductory phrases like: "Discussing salary is always awkward for me, so..." "I know you're eager to know requirements, but..." "Could I say something about that?" Or, "When we discuss money up front I get worried I'll be screened out or boxed in, so could we...?"

To find out what's so important about knowing your salary requirements, use questions like: "I notice we're back on salary again. May I ask you a question?" The employer says okay. You continue, "Are you wondering if you can afford me, or do you just need it for an application, or something else?" Or, "I notice we've come back to salary. I'd like you to know that I'd be glad to talk about money, and even share my tax return with you at some point if it's important, but could we take a moment to talk about why we need to discuss it now?"

Give up. You can disregard my salary-making rules altogether and reveal your salary up front. That will also end a tug of war. You always have that option available, and I even discuss it in Chapter 10. I don't, however, recommend it.

People's attention easily gets focused on the glass-half-empty side of postponing, so they ask, "What if they get angry with me?" Note that the same glass is also half full: "What if they're *more impressed* with me?"

One client reported an incident that happened when he was being interviewed by a recruiter who was retained by a family-owned company. The recruiter's job was to make a good selection and to do it *more objectively* than the family could on its own.

In one group interview the recruiter pressed my client for salary expectations. The client postponed it several times; the family brass were in the room and they were showing some signs of discomfort. The recruiter turned to them and remarked, "This man is doing *exactly* what I would tell a candidate of mine to do in this situation."

He scored points by focusing the interview on contribution, not payback. Check out Daniel's story under the "too low" heading at the beginning of Chapter 6.

Don't worry about upsetting the interviewer, for now; keep reading! Learn rules 2 to 5. If you allow the right mind-set to develop, you'll find your own natural words and ways to postpone salary talk. At the end of the next chapter, I disclose how others have said it, which will help you compose and embrace your own way of postponing salary talk. If you need help coming up with a phrase that suits you, my telecoaching as described in the Coaching and Practice Chapter 12, can make this easy.

Development of an Offer

With the right research and approach, the tactics discussed above can even allow you strategically to explore positions seemingly beneath you.

For instance, I had a client with high-level management capabilities who chose to interview for a line-manager position paying way below his worth. Although normally that would be a waste of time, by applying proper salary-talk timing he was able to develop the interview into a superior offer. Here's his own account.

My interview was with the vice president of operations. He said the slot he wanted to fill was operations manager, salary $35,000. When he asked if that salary would be okay, I said I wanted to table salary discussions until we were sure I was right for the job. Then, while he talked about the company, I made mental notes about its problem areas, to go along with what I'd learned by reading the company literature and talking to the secretary.

He asked what my strengths were, and I told him the top four. He asked what my weaknesses were, and after about a fifteen-second pause I said I'd need additional time to think of a weakness with respect to this position.

After more discussion about my background, which I related to company problem areas, he offered me the position of district manager at a salary of $60,000 to $70,000.

Once again, I declined to discuss salary. Instead I steered the conversation back to four of their stores in South Carolina, which I knew from my research were ineffectively managed. I pointed out qualifications listed on my résumé that coincided with that need.

Then he asked me how much I actually wanted in salary. I answered that I felt my salary should be based on the responsibilities of the job and the standards of the industry. If we got clarity on that, the salary would fall in line.

After that he began talking about an even better job concerning the four problem stores. He said that the job, on approval of the president, could pay $80,000 to $100,000!

An interview that was supposed to take only thirty minutes actually took ninety, and my interviewer said he'd talk to the president about paying top dollar for top people.

Another client deliberately interviewed for an advertised position for which he was overqualified: a manager of computer-aided design (CAD), pegged at $55,000 a year. He followed up the interview with a letter telling how, to save the company untold grief and overhead, he could 1) solve the problems he and the interviewer had talked about, 2) solve some other problems the interviewer had hinted at, and 3) help over the next two years to integrate the CAD with the CAM (computer-aided-manufacturing) systems.

If he had revealed his salary requirements in the beginning, he'd have been screened out while the company was in the **budget** stage and never been hired in the **judgit** stage, at $95,000.

Seller-Buyer Role Reversal in Negotiations: Part I

Finally, common sales sense says you'll get your best money if you wait. An interesting role reversal takes place if you postpone salary discussions until offer time.

Interviews start with employers buying and you selling. If you even passively agree to an X-dollar price or range for the offer, they will line up their candidates, pick one, and say, "Okay, I'll buy you for X dollars." If you postpone discussing salary, however, that role is reversed. They are no longer shoppers, they are sellers. They are in a position where *they* want *you*. They have judged your quality, not your price. They've decided to ask you to join them, so they're selling the job to you! They are motivated at this time to offer you their best price, because they want your contribution. If they aren't beyond the budget stage yet, this is the only time they'll be motivated to break through it.

So be prepared when Mr. Employer looks you in the eye and says, "What sort of salary are you looking for?" Ask yourself whether he's in the judgit stage. Remember that Salary-Making Rule 1 is *Postpone salary discussions until you have been offered the job.*

Chapter 4
Salary-Making Rule 2:
Who Goes First

"What will it take to bring you aboard?" Mr. Employer asks.

"Are you offering me the job?" you say, to delay.

"Yes."

Now what? Should you answer the question? No more delay is necessary; they're ready to make an offer.

Let's calculate the odds of coming out ahead if you go first. Keep in mind that your work and dedication are intangible and difficult to price. That means there's a range. Even if the employer is in the budget phase, there is still a range to work with. Let's say, for example, that the company's range for this job is $50,000 to $55,000. If you go first you can be only, as Goldilocks might tell you, too high, too low, or just right. Let's see what happens.

Calculating Winning Odds of the First Move

You Go First—Too High

You think, "Okay, you dirty, chiseling rats, I know you're out to steal me cheap, but I'm too smart for you." In your most diplomatic tones you say, "I know what I'm worth, and I want $60,000 to accept your offer."

The response? Probably, "Sorry, wrong number."

Your comeback: "Aw, I was just kidding. I really would accept $59,000. Fifty-eight thousand dollars? Fifty-seven thousand dollars sounds reasonable. Fifty-six thousand? Would you believe I love this place so much I'd go as low as $55,000?"

Sound like begging? Awkward, isn't it? So you lose the offer, or beg for the job.

The first of four charts illustrates the win-loss ratio here.

Wins	Losses
0	The Job
	Your Dignity (Begging)

Figure 4-1. You GoFirst—Too High. The Outcome

Actually, the rejection might be phrased like this: "Well, $60,000 is not really the range we were thinking of, so give me some time to talk to our comptroller about it and get back to you, let's say, Thursday." (Don't hold your breath.)

You Go First—Too Low

You think, "Listen, Scrooge, you may get Bob Cratchit for peanuts, but you're paying me a fair wage." Firmly you say, "I know how valuable I am, and I won't touch your job for less than $40,000."

Mr. Employer is disappointed. He thought he was finally getting quality and finds out you are bargain-basement merchandise. "Well," he replies, "that's not really the range we were thinking of, so give me some time to talk to our comptroller about it and get back to you, say, Thursday." (Again, don't hold your breath.)

Or he might say some version of "Sold!" like: "$40,000. Well, that wasn't exactly the range we were thinking of, but I think we can come up with it if you really think you're worth that much. When would you like to start?" (You just got socked for $10,000.)

Wins	Losses
0	The Job
The Job	$5,000 to $10,000

Figure 4-2. You GoFirst—Too Low. The Outcome

You Go First—Just Right

What if you're just right? That is, you happen to hit the top of the range: "This will cost you $55,000, Mr. Employer."

"Well, that wasn't exactly the range we were thinking of," Mr. Employer says, "but I think we could come up with it if you really think you're worth that much. When would you like to start?" Sound familiar? Of course. It's the same words as the "Too low" response. So even if you were just right, you'll always wonder if you really were too low!

Wins	Losses
The Job	$?????

Figure 4-3. You GoFirst—Just Right. The Outcome

So Salary-Making Rule 2 is: *Let them go first.*

If you go first, you can choose from among these outcomes: Lose the job, lose both the job and your dignity, lose $5,000 to $10,000, or lose track of whether you've lost or won. Not very encouraging odds.

Seller-Buyer Role Reversal in Negotiations: Part II

Remember the role reversal? Well, because of that, it's not even your place to go first. If you've followed Salary-Making Rule 1, the interviewer becomes the seller now. It's the seller's responsibility to name the price.

When you go to buy a new suit and find one that's right, you ask, "What's it cost?" Does the seller reply, "Well, how much have you got?" or "What did you pay for your last suit?" It's not *your* job to determine how much this job is worth to these people in this situation at this time. (You do need to know your market value, of course. We'll get to that in Chapter 5.) Employers know their business plans. They should have an idea of how you can make or save them a buck. It's their place to tell you the number.

How to Postpone Salary Talk: Part II

In the play *Harvey*, people were moved by the lost-child look of Elwood P. Dowd to ask, "Is there something I can do for you?" He always replied, "What did you have in mind?" Keep that phrase handy, as in: "Well, I'm sure you have something budgeted for this position. What range did you have in mind?" Or: "I have some idea of the market, but for a moment let's start with your range."

Some interviewers may be very persistent about knowing your range or previous salary. Usually that happens prior to an offer, and this is covered by Salary-Making Rule 1. Remember, discussing salary before an offer is just another way to get you to go first. Here are a few more of the ways you can postpone salary discussions to make sure interviewers go first. I've numbered them to help you pick them out.

[1]Some clients, when asked about present salary, say, "I'm paid very fairly for my responsibilities in my present job, and I expect a fair salary with respect to my responsibilities here." Then continue by saying (if there's been no offer yet), "Let's keep

talking to make sure I'm the one you want," or (if an offer has been made) "What did you have in mind?"

[2]When asked the second or third time for his salary, one client of mine finally just ignored it. [3]A second said, "Hell, it don't make no diff'rence what I was a-makin' b'fore. It's what *you're* gonna pay me that counts, ain't it?"

[4]A third client took up the issue head on. "Maybe you've noticed by now that it's a clear principle of mine never to discuss salary up front. If we're going to work together, we'll have to respect each other's principles, won't we? So let's see how I can help you make [or save] money."

Another client, when questioned by a personnel representative about his present salary said, [5]"I don't have to answer that, do I?" "No," the personnel rep replied, "I just have to ask it."

The best postponing phrase speaks *confidence* in being hired. [6]For example: "I'm sure we can come to a good salary agreement when the time comes." Often your interviewer will be set at ease by a statement like this [7]"Don't worry about salary; I know I need to make you more than I cost. Let's make sure the fit is right."

If you have some experience of your own as an interviewer, you could say [8]"Look, if salary is all you're worried about, there's no problem! When I've hired people myself, salary has been just the finishing touch to the person who can really play for the team. Let's talk about it when we're sure I'm the player you're after."

Here are some additional examples that show you can invent your own phrases rather than reciting someone else's.

[9]Nancy, who had been underpaid in a previous position and had run her own business for two years, handled salary questions this way: "I don't want to appear difficult. I can understand that you want to be sure you can afford me, and I won't require a salary out of line with the job. But it is a principle of mine not to discuss salary yet, because it can throw us off track. What's really

important is whether I'm right for the job and what I can produce for you."

When Denny was asked his salary expectations, he replied [10]"Well, compensation is about number three on my priorities list right now. Number one is making sure we can work together, and I'd just as soon concentrate on that for now, if you don't mind." Denny was able to boost the employer's limit of "$60,000, tops" to $85,000 and bonuses!

After her boss declared, "Raises will be five percent across the board this year," Helen said [11]"I'm not interested in discussing raises yet. First, let's make sure our goals match up. Then if we need to figure out raises, we'll have something to go on." Instead of a 5-percent raise, Helen got a new **judgit** salary, 18 percent higher than her old one, to go with a new job title and responsibilities.

Diana Jackson, an outstanding career consultant in New York, reports the following response was successful for one of her clients [12]"I wouldn't want to say anything at this point that might scare you away, and I'm sure you don't want to say anything that might discourage me, so if it's okay with you, I'd like to just keep an open mind on the subject for now."

Tim, who earned well into six figures in real estate, was exploring a passion of his — privatization within public education. He knew there would be no point in trying to hide his previous earnings, since one look at the title and level of responsibility in his previous position would tell an employer he'd been in the upper bracket. So, instead of attempting to camouflage it, he tackled it head on. When asked, "What did you make there?" he smiled knowingly and said [13]"A lot!" Pause. Then he finished with, "Probably more than I'd make here, but don't worry, salary isn't my main concern." This way he was able to negotiate top dollar without being screened out as too expensive.

Barbara was in a slightly different situation; she'd had salaries all over the board and knew that information wouldn't really help an employer. So she handled it by telling Human

Resources [14]"I know you need this salary history, and I'd be glad to tell you. First, let me explain why I didn't put it on the application: I didn't think it would help us very much to get to a reasonable offer. You see, I've had consulting projects that would annualize to $120,000 a year, and I've worked in pay-the-rent type jobs in the $30s. I have some salary research relevant to this position which I can bring in when we're ready to talk seriously. I think it will be much more informative. I don't think we'll have much problem with salary when that time comes."

[15]One of my favorite post-offer responses, but a bit too flippant for practical use is: "Me, mention a figure first? I have absolutely no upper limits. Now, what did you have in mind?"

Want more samples? Go to www.SalaryNegotiations.com and you'll find more. Use BoughtTheBook as a password.

So you can see, you have some choice and some leeway in Mr. Employer's office.

Let's just say he's offered you the job and urged you to say what salary you'll accept. Since you know that there's nothing to gain by going first, you've confidently asked him to name his opening bid.

Sure enough, he drums his fingers on the desk, clears his throat, and states a price. Now it's your move again. What do you do? You follow Salary-Making Rule 3.

Chapter 5
Salary-Making Rule 3:
Your First Response

In my job as a career consultant, in which almost everything I do is individualized and there are exceptions to every rule, it's delightful to know that Salary-Making Rule 3 always holds. Salary-Making Rule 3 is When you hear the figure or range, repeat the figure or top of the range, and then be quiet.

Dangers and Power of Silence: Out for the Count

You must repeat the figure or top of the range with a contemplative tone in your voice as if this were the start of a multinational summit meeting. Your enthusiasm for the job and company and industry has been unbounded up to this point. Now let a quiet look of concern grace your countenance and gaze at your slightly shuffling feet as you ponder this offer. Count to thirty and think.

Quickly Calculate the Annualized Amount

First, you should calculate roughly what the offer is in annual terms. Hourly workers can easily convert an hourly figure to a yearly one by doubling it in thousands. So fifteen dollars an hour is roughly $30,000 a year; twenty dollars an hour, $40,000; all based on forty hours a week with no overtime. To go from weekly to yearly, multiply by fifty (or divide by two and add two zeros). For instance, $600 a week is $30,000 a year, and so on.

Calculate what the salary is, then compare it with your expectations of what this job should pay, considering your quality. During this time there is silence in the room. If you had not repeated the figure or the top of the range, the silence would be awkward or dangerous. Your interviewer would wonder if you had gone to sleep or if you'd heard what was said. The interviewer might think you were accepting it or that you're too shy to talk about money.

But when you repeat it, the interviewer knows that you heard it and fears you're disappointed. Let the interviewer be nervous, worried, or anxious. That's okay for 30 seconds. That way he or she will again consider your quality and the return you would make on the company's investment.

What Happens When You're Quiet

The most likely outcome of this silence is a raise. How about that! You haven't been on the job for even thirty seconds and already you have a raise. It might sound like "[silence] But we could go as high as X dollars for someone like you" or "[silence] But we could be flexible on that." If you like, you can greet the raise with the same silent treatment: "$60,000. Hmmm [silence]."

Sometimes you'll get an explanation of why the budget allows only that much. "Times are rough, competition's tough. We've just sunk money into an updated Flam-a-doodle Wig Whumper, and the cash flow is squeezed by the president's frequent business trips to exotic locations."

Listen. Be quiet. Think.

Compare, contrast, evaluate, and then respond.

What do you respond with? The truth.

Figure 5-2. Let a quiet look of concern grace your countenance as you ponder the offer. Count to thirty and think.

Responding with the Truth

The truth is either "Sounds great," "Sounds acceptable," or "Sounds disappointing." You'll know which one is correct because before the interview you'll have followed the advice in this chapter and researched your market value. That will give you the strength and power to negotiate for your full value because you'll have the information to back it up. (The same approach applies to raise negotiating.)

Note that your past or present salary is only one indication of your market value. Earlier you learned not to let your most recent salary restrict your new one. You might have sidestepped or postponed the salary question altogether by asserting, "all I expect is a fair and competitive offer with respect to this job."

So, now, even if this offer is *less* than your most recent salary, you must abide by the same rules. It's not fair to complain, "But that's less than I'm earning now," or "That's less than I earned before." While employers usually try to exceed your previous salary, your salary in *some other job* does not really determine the value of your work in *this* job – that value is made up from a formula with three components.

So don't compare the offer with your most recent salary. Instead, use the thirty seconds to compare their offer with your research, using the formula below.

Formula

How do you determine your fair market value?

First understand that a fair market value is not one neat, tidy number, but a range. It's the answer to the question "Within what range would a company have to pay to find someone like you?" Or similarly, "If *you* don't take the job, what will the company need to offer someone as good as you to take it?"

A market value is a composite picture made up of three pieces: your Objectively Researched Value (ORV$), your extra Individual Value (IV$), and what I'll call your Risk-factor Dollars (Rf$).

You left-brained folks might think of it as a formula in which the market value equals the sum of three other values:

Market Value = ORV\$ + IV\$ + Rf\$.

For you right-brained, visual types, just think "present, past, future," and picture your market value as a composite photograph made by combining these three perspectives: the *present* going rate

(ORV$), the added value of your accumulated *past* experience (IV$), and your *future* contribution (Rf$).

Left- or right-brained, in order to fully understand these formulas, you need some definitions.

ORV$ (Objectively Researched Value); present. Objectively researched information from current published data about the going rate; this year's average earning range for people doing the kind of work you're considering.

IV$ (Individual Value); past. A subjective assessment of the strength of your past track record as it applies to this new job or promotion. It puts you somewhere on a scale from entry level to seasoned professional, possibly with a unique competitive advantage. IV$ measures how you stack up individually above or below the competition.

RF$ (Risk-Factor Dollars); future. Compensation you are willing to make contingent on your future success; speculative compensation.

Calculating the Three Factors, Part I: ORV$

E-Resources

In the days before the internet, researching your competitive value required a trip to the library only to discover dusty books with data so far out of date you needed a scientific calculator to gross up by three years' compounded inflation to come up with meaningful numbers. By contrast, www.PayScale.com collects up-to-the-minute salary data from thousands of individuals every day.

Very precise salary-research data is available to you today at the speed of light that would have cost thousands of dollars just a few years ago. The problem is, the same alacrity that put these sites up can also send them into obsolescence.

Websites sprout, grow, blossom and then either they continually re-invest, re-invent themselves or they become eclipsed by an even-better-yet technology.

Frankly, it's hard for the printed page to keep up with e-resources! So I encourage you to consult my website for a continually updated list and critique of web-based resources. www.SalaryNegotiations.com

ORV$ (Objectively Researched Value)

Find out in what range people get paid for work similar to yours by consulting published surveys. Make sure you're comparing apples to apples, that the salary you find matches the responsibilities of the job you expect to be paid for.

People often have a hard time matching their job to a job title. You'll need to pick one – or two, perhaps – that seem close. Where there are actual job descriptions along with the titles, that can help you select a title most closely related to the level of responsibility.

Once you're on track with a title and perhaps a job description, begin collecting pay-comparison-analysis information that will coalesce into your objectively researched value (ORV$). You have five resources, which are not exclusive of one another:

- library and other printed information,
- internet resources: online information,
- library-research-for-computer-dummies technique,
- person-to-person research: direct-dial resources, and
- person-to-person research: word-of-mouth resources.

Library and Other Printed Information

Frankly, while there is printed salary info you can unearth in the stacks of your local library, you don't need to plow through those stacks anymore. For all practical purposes, your library's computer room with Google will give you more than enough data to affix a range to your ORV$.

Internet Resources: Online Information

The four "preferred providers"

In the following pages you'll find screen shots and more in-depth information on my "Favorite Four" sites. They are, namely:

- www.JobStar.org

- www.PayScale.com

- www.Salary.com, and

- www.CareerJournal.com

You'll also find brief information on other sites of relevance. Since the world of cyberspace is ever changing, you'll be reminded several times, too, that you can go to my website www.SalaryNegotiations.com for the latest update on e-resources. Some info might be password protected, reserved for people-like you-who purchased my book; try BoughtTheBook.

JobStar Central

Job Search Guide
from your local public library

JobStar Central

- Resumes
- Career Guides
- Salary Info
- Hidden Jobs
- Ask Electra
- Search Site

For LOCAL Job Ads & Career Help, Visit these LOCAL JobStars!

CALIFORNIA
- Los Angeles
- Sacramento
- San Diego
- San Francisco

NATIONAL

WORLDWIDE

Contents
Questionnaire
Reviews
About JobStar

E-mail Electra

Free Job Seeker Tools
Search 200,000 Jobs and Companies Free
Career Test and Resume Post

Jobs - Find a Job Today
Search New Jobs & Candidates by Industry
-Employment Opportunities

Ads by Gooooooogle

GET READY

"How To" Information for Job Seekers Everywhere: Resumes, Career & Salary Info, Hidden Job Market

Resumes
How to write them & where to send them. "What's the Right Resume for Me?" and Sample Resumes & Cover Letters

Career Guides
Whether you're starting, continuing or changing...you need information to plan your next move..including Free Online Career Tests.

Salary Info
Links to over 300 selected general and professional Salary Surveys on the Web from "Accounting" to "Warehousing."

Hidden Job Market
The best jobs are never advertised: here's a step by step plan to help you find the best job for you. Includes a guide to Researching Companies.

Ask Electra
Your personal electronic librarian and frequently asked questions such as "How do I handle a request for a salary history?"

The Motherlode of Salary Surveys

GET TO WORK

Looking for a job or planning a career? You're in the right place for job openings & career help for California and beyond.

CALIFORNIA

LOCAL Job Ads - Job Fairs - Career Centers & MORE

- JobStar Los Angeles
- JobStar Sacramento
- JobStar San Diego
- JobStar San Francisco

NATIONAL
- JobStar Executive
Information on job hunting and career management from The *Wall Street Journal* and other respected sources.
- JobStar Job Bank
A searchable database of 30,000+ middle- to senior-level positions that is updated daily.

WORLDWIDE
- JobStar Asia
From the *Asian Wall Street Journal* and *FarEastern Economic Review*.
- JobStar Europe
From the *Wall Street Journal Europe*.

Figure 5-1. JobStar.org

Favorite #1: JobStar.org

Nothing beats JobStar for getting to the source of the data! And free! It's been around since the 80s, and its founder, Mary Ellen Mort, pioneered one-stop shopping for salary surveys: compensation data published by associations, recruitment firms, government departments, schools, research organizations, etc. It has about 80 categories for salary information with links to over 300 sites.

If you're looking for clout in your negotiations, (i.e., you want to show your potential employer your research) these surveys in their "straight from the horse's mouth" format could be a bit more compelling to an employer than generic information compiled by a third party.

For instance, an advertising executive that points to a survey from Advertising Age Magazine is using a reference the Hiring Decision Maker already knows is credible. Use these to bolster the believability of your other online research from sites like the one at left.

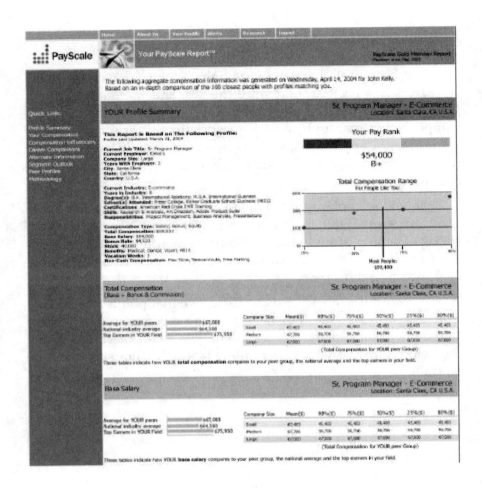

Figure 5-2. PayScale.com

Favorite #2: PayScale.com

Nothing beats PayScale for "up to the minute" salary information. Unlike other services that get their data second-hand, PayScale continuously collects compensation information directly from real people.

Since 2002 PayScale has been running the largest real-time salary survey on the web, collecting tens-of-thousands of individual salary profiles each month. These profiles enable PayScale to provide highly relevant information about what an individual should be paid based on their unique personal job profile (job title, skills, experience, location, etc.).

Their sophisticated proprietary software assures accurate high-quality data, and unlike most for-profit salary sites built to supply Human Resources departments of large companies with information, PayScale's service was built with the individual in mind from the get-go.

Good information is available for free and their purchased info is very well done and job-hunter/user friendly.

Readers of this book can access a special PayScale page, if you go to www.PayScale.com/1000minute.

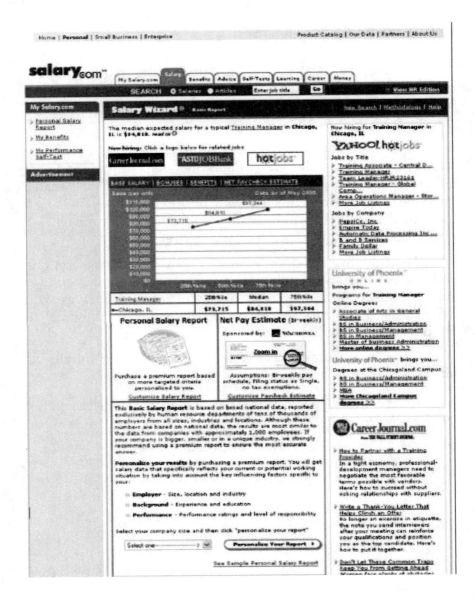

Figure 5-3. Salary.com

Favorite #3: Salary.com

Salary.com is the oldest commercial internet site for salary data. Originally designed with HR department in mind, it now offers info to individuals. It reports that in 2005, more than 2.4 million unique monthly visitors out of a U.S. workforce of 142.5 million. Salary.com estimates that 1 employee in 5 has viewed salary information at its site in the past year. Like Payscale, this is a for-profit site.

Freebies include a general report on your salary, based on a company size of 1000 people; a more detailed report is available, of course, and reasonably priced, too. More updates and critique available online at my website: www.SalaryNegotiations.com.

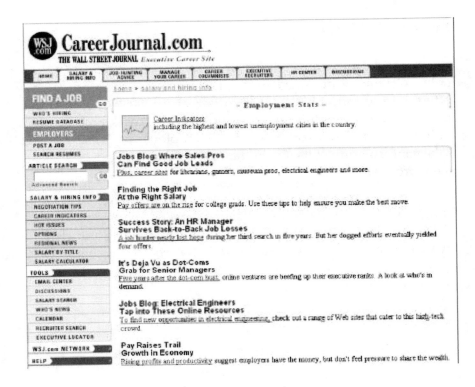

Figure 5-4. CareerJournal.com

Favorite #4: CareerJournal.com [Wall Street Journal]

In addition to charts of salaries (likely from the same primary sources you can find through JobStar.org) the Wall Street Journal's site will link you to articles on different industries to help you get a fix on your ORV$. Go to its home page and click on a tab marked "Salary & Hiring Info."

CareerJournal.com is a major internet career site for executives, managers and professionals. The site's job database offers more than 100,000 available positions, including job listings in the CareerJournal National Network. Sometimes you can get Salary information in a posted listing here (or at Monster.com, etc.) for a job similar to yours.

CareerJournal's unlimited JobSeek Agents will alert candidates whenever a job is added that matches their criteria.

Through the daily updates and thousands of archived articles, you can examine hiring demand and salary data for a vast array of industries and job functions, and access information on all aspects of job hunting and career management. Editorial features include more than a dozen noted columnists; a wide range of features to help with resume writing, interviewing, networking and negotiating a new job offer, as well as in-depth guidance on improving your current career.

Other Sites of interest. Check www.SalaryNegotiations.com for updates on these websites:

SalaryExpert.com: says you can compare executive salaries at half-dozen companies of comparable size, which it will find for you. Such a tool is valuable for job hunters, and also for boards' CEO search committees and pay panels.

Vault.com: particularly enticing because it can have salary information as precise as the exact company you're interested it, but by the same token, it's spotty, you have to join to get anything worthwhile here. It has a job board, too.

SalaryPower.com: A new site that says it's mission is to enhance the employment relationship between employees and employers by developing a web site that offers accurate, reliable compensation data to improve compensation discussions. Not functional as of this printing; check my website for further info.

SEC.gov has all the 10-K, annual and quarterly reports, etc., on publicly traded companies. The officers and top executive salaries are plain for all to see (with a little digging). You can find their company-specific search engine page at: www.sec.gov/edgar/searchedgar/companysearch.html

Computerjobs.com: Industry specific site with salary information. The info here is garnered from employees' own report of their earnings, but without the quality-assurance of the type of software PayScale.com has, so the salary info may not be as reliable. When you find these sites through Google and JobStar.org, don't rely on them solely – your best reliability is found in the four favorites.

WageAccess.com: The WageAccess™ Compensation Survey is a multi-industry salary survey that includes over 500 benchmark positions and ensures complete participant confidentiality. Alternatively, participants can purchase the Advanced Survey Results which include a variety of descriptive statistics, compensation analysis tools and salary trends, and allows results to be queried, selected and filtered by geographic location, industry and/or company size.

LinkedIn.com—a new kind of research tool. This isn't primarily a salary info site, however, as an e-networking site, you can use it to get salary information when you're very targeted. Just follow their "networking" protocols and find another person to talk to who works or worked for the company you're interested in, or who has a job similar to yours. Explore the pros and cons of this, and other sites like it, in the *"Person-to-Person Research"* section below.

Library-Research-For-Computer-Dummies Technique

I assume most of you are computer savvy and comfortable accessing internet information, but if you're at all intimidated by the bits and bytes world, try my library-research-for-computer-dummies technique. Many libraries have a telephone information line you can call to have a human being (you remember those, don't you?) look up information you want from print or electronic sources.

In fact, if you walk in, there's a whole army of librarians who'll help you not just with salary research, but the whole vast array of job hunting services and help online. Your tax dollars at work, eh? Take advantage of it.

Computer Resources: Rent a Nerd

For more complicated searches, or if you simply prefer to delegate the work, consider hiring someone else do the work for you, especially if your job responsibilities are unique. (I know a couple people who will do this for you—email me at jkchapman@aol.com, or visit my website for referrals to research helpers.) Salary information pegged to job titles can be off the mark if your position requires you to wear many hats. Having a real person dig out the information you want could be a wise investment.

Person-to-Person Research: Direct-Dial and Internet Networking Resources.

You can just pick up the phone and conduct your own private survey. Call people doing work like yours. Tell them you're doing a salary survey and that you'll be happy to share your findings with them when you're done if they'll participate. Ask what the range is in their company for the job in question. Carry through with your promise to send results to them.

If you don't want to call, you can write. Use web research on company websites for names/email addresses of appropriate people for your survey, or join and use the recently developed e-networking sites.

E-networking through sites like LinkedIn, Ryze, Friendster, Spoke, EntreMate, and others can be a more modern way to make these personal connections. These sites are set up to facilitate networking among their members. You can search the membership to find fellow professionals at your level who might participate in your survey, or who might have specific knowledge of the salary ranges you're researching.

Once again, visit my website (with BoughtTheBook password, if needed) www.SalaryNegotiations.com for recent developments in this arena. Online e-networking for job-related leads, information (like salary), connections, etc, is still in its infancy—poised for either a spectacular take-off or a dismal fizzle.

Example of Person to Person Direct Dial/Internet

Let's say you're interviewing for a position as a purchasing manager for an urban hospital. Pick out six places that would have similar customer service positions: perhaps a medical clinic, a for-profit hospital, a nonprofit denominational hospital, a unionized company, and the local headquarters for a medium-size chain of stores. Pick companies in your or a similar location.

Ask to talk to their purchasing managers. Explain to those people that you're negotiating for a position similar to theirs and name the responsibilities. Tell them that you're calling five people from their city to learn comparable salary ranges, and that if they participate in your survey you'll be glad to send them the results.

You might wish to explain that you'll only send the info to the five (or so) participants and company names won't be mentioned, only the categories, like "nonprofit denominational hospital." Ask, "Within what range would this position pay in your organization?" They'll participate if they're curious about their own positions and their own worth in the open market.

You can also request the same information from company personnel representatives if you prefer to talk with them. They may be more reluctant to divulge their companies' private pay information; on the other hand, they may be more motivated to know the results of your research, because it's free, and they can use it in their work.

The advantage of this method is that you get up-to-the-minute, precise salary information tailored exactly to your location. The disadvantage is that the sample is so small that you might get skewed information.

Person-to-Person Research: Word-of-Mouth Resources

Besides association members, sources of money-talk outside the library include recruiters, employment agents, personnel professionals, and your own network.

Recruiters, job and career counselors, outplacement counselors, and employment-agency counselors are all good sources of wage and earnings data. Recruiters generally specialize in a certain area of the job market, so you'd want to talk to one who knows your niche. The other counselors deal with a wide variety of clients, so their input won't be as detailed, but they are likely to know something about many different types of positions.

Ask around until you find someone who knows one of those professionals (or someone who knows someone who knows) and call that person.

Read the section in the Special Situations chapter (Chapter 8) about discussing salary at networking interviews. Your network can give you not only information about salary ranges, but also advice to determine where you fit within those ranges. Does that concept ring a bell? It should. It is the second factor in the formula I gave you earlier, your extra Individual Value, IV$.

Calculating the Three Factors, Part II: IV$

IV$, Extra Individual Value

IV$ refers to your assessment of how well (or poorly) you can do the work compared with other candidates' ability. Are you a cut above average? Well known? Have a special expertise? If so, your added value can add dollars to put your salary in the above-average range. Here are some examples.

- A salesman, Tom, sold safety equipment to manufacturing companies. Besides sales ability (which every candidate had), he had ten years of cultivating his network through lunches, golf games, plant tours, birthday cards, and other contact-building activities. When Tom called a company, he could count on a face-to-face appointment. This IV$ enabled him to negotiate a higher commission.

- Ben, a paralegal, applied for a job revitalizing a small specialty-law library. He was overqualified for the $35,000 position. By reinterpreting this "overqualified" to mean "having double the IV$ of other candidates," he doubled the offer in a unique way. He accepted the budgeted $35,000, but did the job (and then some) in only twenty hours a week. Existing clerical personnel whom he trained covered the other twenty hours. So his employer got 150 percent of what had been hoped for, Ben got $70,000 annualized earnings, and the $35,000 budget was maintained.

- Beth, an administrative assistant, was very familiar with Cougar Mountain accounting software. She added $3,000 IV$ to her market range because the company had budgeted $3,000 to train a new hire in this software.

- A doctor was well known for his abilities in dealing with allergies. He had published a book about it. The clinic he was joining could expect to see many more allergy patients because of his reputation, and additional business from those patients' families; he added this IV$ to his objectively researched value.

IV$ can be a negative number. If you're below average, entry level, lacking a specific requirement, etc., your objectively researched value can be adjusted downward to make you competitively priced.

A teacher switched careers to enter sales. Even though in her estimation she could give sales gurus Zig Ziglar and Joe Girard a run for their money, she was unproven in the eyes of the world. By keeping her salary expectations at the lower end of the objectively researched value, she remained competitive. She was content to reap her big rewards in year two when she expected, as Zig would say, "to see you — at the top."

An IBM mainframe programmer interviewed for an MIS quality-assurance position, a big jump for him. He didn't know the new programming language or hardware very well, but he convinced the employer that his learning curve would be short. He was willing to accept a few thousand below average for the position in exchange for the job and a six-month salary review.

To go into business for himself, a public-utility employee left a position where he'd worked with many users of the network he managed. He decided to go into business for himself as a PC consultant helping consumers with Windows and basic computer software problems. Best Buy charged $60-$125 an hour, a good benchmark for ORV$. But, since he needed to establish his reputation first he started by offering his first hour's consultation free and 25 percent off the hourly rate after that, a good example of how circumstances might make your IV$ a negative number.

Two resources for identifying your IV$:

- Me. When people call me for telecoaching, there's often IV$ negotiating strengths they're not aware of. I am often able to help them see their IV$ in their mind so they can negotiate well and eventually see in their paycheck. Call me if you wish. See Chapter 12.

- My website. There's more examples of IV$s in a password-protected area on my website (BoughtTheBook). You're welcome to visit and learn. www.SalaryNegotiations.com

Calculating the Three Factors, Part III: Rf$

Rf$, Risk-factor Dollars

Objectively Researched Value determines a range, and Individual Value a place within that range. Rf$ can take the salary off the chart! Whenever you are willing to negotiate compensation contingent on performance, you add what I call Risk-factor Dollars (Rf$).

Employers' basic principle in hiring (and conversely, firing) is Tom Jackson's Make Me a Buck principle. They bring you aboard only because they think your contribution will pay back more money than your cost.

How much more money? Goo gobs? Are you willing to bet on it?

If so, then you can add Rf$ to your value.

If you're just another cog in the wheel, you may not have much solid Rf$ value to work with, but on the other hand, if you expect to make a direct impact on the bottom line, this value could be very high.

Rf$ Illustration: emergencies.

Emergency situations are a good example. My client Walter knew that the company he was interviewing with was about to lose an advertising account worth about $100,000 profit each year, and he was the knight in shining armor who would rescue it. He had a shot at adding a hefty bonus to his compensation. His IV$

was much the same as the next candidate's, but he was available right away, and the company was behind the eight ball! If the customer didn't get a new account manager immediately, they'd put the account out for proposal to other agencies. He added $20,000 "rescue" Rf$ to his objectively researched value.

Rf$ Illustration: Stock Options.

Stock options are another good example of Rf$ compensation.

New ventures also have potentially high Rf$. If you're hired to spearhead an upgrade of a company's website, from a passive site to one that could open up gates for a flood of money to pour in, you can negotiate a piece of that new pie. If you take part of your compensation in performance bonuses and commissions, those added Rf$ could make your value jump considerably. I devote a complete chapter, Chapter 11, to understanding and negotiating stock options.

Rf$ Illustration: other.

Direct contributions to increased sales, improved quality, enhanced public image, higher visibility, innovative new product lines, better conference results, etc., are all things that can be measured. Because they can be measured, you can negotiate additional compensation based on performance. So it pays to try to predict the future and add it to your market value.

Timing

A note about timing. Research and calculate your market value at any time. It's a good thing to do even at the very beginning of the job search and interviewing process, but you should delay actual discussions about IV$ and Rf$ components until the employer is serious enough to make you an offer. There's a fine line here. You do want to ferret out information in the interview to help you determine your IV$ and Rf$, but *you do not want to discuss them yet as items of compensation.*

In the beginning, just reassure the employer you'll be fine with a "fair market value." Later, when you're talking turkey, negotiate those pieces of your market value.

Your Own Opinion of Where You Fit

Mary-Ellen Mort, a developer of the JobStar web page, has words of wisdom I quote here:

"Obviously the more you can find out (from your network, your research on the company and the industry) the more you are able to guess what your skills can mean to the company. Inside information—such as they stand to lose a contract if they don't get someone who knows how to do X—is the key.

"The interviewing process itself is one of the best ways of nosing out such stuff. Ask the right questions; listen for the answers. Check out the impressions you get during the interview with your close and confidential network. Often they can add something that was not said about the vacancy or the need or the players involved.

"This is one of the big reasons you should delay the salary talk till later in the game. Often people say it's because you want them to want you [first, before you discuss salary].

"That's true of course.

"But the more you talk and schmooze and listen between the words, the more you have a sense of how much they need you and what it will cost them if they don't have you. Job seekers forget they are not just giving info in the interviews, they are collecting it too."

Her point is expressed well.

Remember the **budget**, **fudgit**, and **judgit** stages? Remember how I encouraged you to postpone salary talk until they are in the **judgit** stage? Well here's where it pays off! In the **judgit** stage, not only do they appreciate your value, but you know your value, too, especially the IV$ and Rf$ values.

Any doubts you had while reading Chapter 2 about delaying salary talk, and how it is only logical to wait until the **judgit** stage to discuss value, should be gone by now. You should now be more confidently grounded in how your value depends on the organization's needs and how those needs and your value often aren't clear until the **judgit** stage.

When, at the **budget** stage, an employer asks your salary expectations, it's logical to say, "I couldn't possibly tell you what I'm worth to you until I know the whole job and how much I can produce for your organization." You may have thoroughly researched your ORV$ market value but, until the **judgit** stage arrives, your understanding of your IV$ and Rf$ value to the firm is incomplete.

Here is an example.

I had a client who applied for a job as a word processor, with a market value of fifteen to eighteen dollars an hour. When asked at the start of the interview if eighteen dollars an hour was acceptable, she *thought*, "Wow! Top of the range!" But she *said*, "If eighteen dollars an hour is a fair and motivating wage, of course it's acceptable, but I'd rather wait and discuss salary when we're both clear about what I can produce for you."

They continued talking. By the time the employer reached **judgit**, it was evident to both of them that, besides needing help with word processing, the company also needed someone who could organize mailing lists, distribute newsletters, deal with printers, and handle a marathon monthly production weekend that required extreme efficiency, patience, and coordination and communication talents.

As a word processor, my client might have been worth just ten to fifteen dollars an hour. But by adding those other responsibilities, she was worth much more. When she postponed money talk until the **judgit** stage, not only did her employer see that increased worth, but so did she!

Ready, Set, Go!

So before you show up at Mr. Employer's office, you should have an opinion — not chiseled in stone — of your range around the range, the highest value you think you're worth, and the lowest you'll accept.

If you have black-and-white evidence to support your opinion, bring it with you in case you want to educate your interviewer. Also, be prepared to upgrade it according to the particulars of the job.

You now have adequate information for responding to a salary offer.

Chapter 6
Salary-Making Rule 4:
Your Researched Response

Going for Top of the Mark

Grounded in your knowledge of the market value for the position and your ultimate knowledge of your quality, you've calculated two figures before going into the interview: the highest you're worth and the lowest you'll accept. So after silence, and perhaps your first raise, tell the interviewer whether the figure offered is too high, too low, or just right.

Salary-Making Rule 4 is *Counter their offer with your researched response.*

Your strategy here is to get your top figure in a way the employer thinks is fair.

Responding to the Offer

Too High

This is generally a pleasant problem, but it deserves more attention than you might think. Remember, you're not out to get every penny you can; you want only a fair salary to match your peak performance. If your employer is making the mistake of overpaying you, the company will begin to feel ripped off, just as you would in the underpaid-vicious-cycle scenario in Chapter 1. Your employer will regret the deal and resent you in the long run. Although you may be delighted with the first paycheck, eventually you'll find yourself trapped because you can't get another job without a pay cut, and you can't get promoted because your boss begrudges your cost already.

The other possibility is that you're unwittingly in over your head. If you expected twenty grand and you're offered forty, maybe you've impressed these folks beyond your capabilities. Although eight hundred dollars a week looks nice, it could turn out to be more like eight hundred dollars for one frustrating week before you're back out on the street.

A response to "Too high" might be: "Well, that's very fair, actually a wonderful offer. I take it as an indication of your belief that I'm someone who can do the job. Let's get the benefits clear and I think we can make the deal."

Finish up the negotiations but provide yourself with time, as suggested in Chapter 7, before you finally accept the position. You'll need that time to make a special effort to research the position, both to make sure you can handle it and to find out why they're being so generous.

A client called me one day deliriously high with an offer equal to a 150-percent salary increase and a benefits package that totaled a 200-percent raise. I was worried. The job seemed okay, but I told him to go back and check it out.

The employer was frank: "We believe high-tech corporations succeed because of teamwork and dedication. Our projects often take years to complete, and they keep us at the cutting edge of technical application. When we find people we like, we want them for the long haul; we don't want our people looking for other positions. We need 100 percent of your energy and commitment, and we know we have to pay for it." Fine! Since we know the employer is happy, we're happy. It's a win-win situation, and we've negotiated right.

Too Low

When the offer is too low, don't give up! There are many ways to increase it. Your first response should be to acknowledge it. "Thirty-five thousand dollars. I appreciate your offer, Mr. Employer." Then refocus on your interest in the job: "And I'd love to work here." Then put out a statement you can both agree on: "And I'm sure you want to pay me a compensation that is fair and will keep me committed and productive, isn't that right?" (What can he say?)

"Well," you continue, "from my research I estimate that positions like this for someone with my qualifications are paying in the range of X to Y thousand dollars. What can you do in that range?"

The range you give will bracket the high end of your research. If your research uncovered a range of $45,000 to $48,000, bracket the high range by saying, "In the range of $47,000 to $50,000."

Typically, your interviewer will respond by telling you what the company can do in that range: something, nothing, whatever. You're ready to continue an honest discussion in order to reach a common ground. Do your best here. Hold on to your researched worth and keep talking to find a way to work it out so you both win. Keep a mutuality about the negotiations. Look for a compensation that is both fair and will keep you committed and productive.

Notice how this negotiation compares with the *You go first – too-high/too-low* scenarios. In either of those cases you could lose the job. Here you have a firm job offer at X thousand dollars. If all further negotiating comes to nothing, you can't lose the job offer. You can always in the end say, "Well, let's go with X dollars" or "No thanks." But it's *your* decision.

Sincere negotiations, in my experience, end up with a satisfying common ground 90 percent of the time.

Many people, though, think they'll lose an employer's respect if they talk very long about money. That's true *before* an offer, as we learned from Salary-Making Rule 1, but after an offer it can actually increase respect.

Too Low – Daniel's Story

For example, Daniel, one of my clients, received an offer on the phone, but insisted on discussing it in person. After two hours of negotiating, he had an acceptable offer. He made an extra $10,000 a year in those two hours. The employer concluded the session with the comment: "If I had any doubts about you before, they are gone now. I *know* why I've hired you." My client had listened carefully to their opinions and offer, and had kept going back to a *researched* response.

Here's where your research and your own estimate of your quality comes into play. If you use PinPoint or any other salary-research method, you may wish to share your findings with your (prospective) employer. Seeing facts on paper might move him to agree more easily to your requests.

If you research a salary spread of $5,000, you'll want to ask for the top of the spread if you believe your expertise merits it. Otherwise, you'll settle for a middle range. Even if you're entry level, however, go for a grand or two above the bottom. Sell your ambition and potential.

Whatever you do, don't say no in the room!

If you can't reach a mutually satisfying salary, you still have the lower offer. Let the employer sweat a little. Remember, the company wants you. Tell the interviewer that you're still very excited about the opportunity and that you both will want to think about it and talk again tomorrow or Friday.

Too Low – wrapping up the interview

Leaving negotiations when the offer is too low puts you in jeopardy of losing the offer altogether. Employers may want to just scrap the whole thing rather than risk hiring you today, only to wave good-bye in a few months when you leave for more money. Make sure they'll honor their current offer while you consider it. You don't want any interlopers to push their way into consideration. If they'll hold to their offer during the negotiations, you've got nothing to lose!

However, you'll need to make a deal: If they'll keep it open, on their part, then on *your* part, you need to reassure them that you'll give them an honest-to-goodness yes or no the next time you meet. And if it's a yes, you mean it.

Say something like this, "Well, we seem far apart at the moment. I don't want to decline the offer because I still think the fit is good. Why don't we do this… Let's talk again soon [means 24 hours or less, BTW]. I'll make you this promise: I'll look over the compensation to see if I can accept it; meanwhile, you can take some time to see if there's anything we've overlooked to make it better. Then, if I can accept that offer, I'll say yes, and I'll mean yes. If I can't feel right about the deal, I'll say no, and suggest you look for another candidate who will fill the bill for you at that price. How does that sound?"

If you don't offer this type of reassurance, they might rescind the offer *even if they said they'd hold it for a day.*

Too Low: bolstering an offer with bennies.

As you will see when you look over the list of bennies and perks in Chapter 7, there may be ways to make the compensation package correct even if the base isn't what you expected. Negotiating profit sharing, bonuses, stock options, vacation time, accelerated-commission scales, an entertainment budget, training budget, tuition reimbursement, or a company car is a way to build your compensation. You or the company may need time to come up with the creative financing.

Just Right

This is unlikely. The first figure you hear is generally the employer's lowest. Even if the interviewer is in a fit of ecstasy and fudging and judging to entice you into the company, prudent business people wouldn't back themselves into a corner. But if it does happen, and you're confident that you've researched correctly, take the same thirty seconds to think about it, then say, "Your figure matches my research exactly. I think that's a perfect starting point. Since I expect to learn fast, work hard, and become very productive for you, I'd like to discuss scheduling a tentative raise to X thousand dollars in six months." That way you're not pushing for anything more than a fair salary, but still bringing up a potential raise.

Remember all the losses we counted in Chapter 4 when you go first? Let's look at the scorecard this time. What a difference when, after letting the interviewer go first, you count to thirty, then counter the company's offer with your researched response.

These "They Go First" winning results are summarized in the table on the following page.

Rule 4: Your Researched Response

Let Them Go First ScoreCard

	Wins	Losses
Too High	The Offer The Job	_____ _____
Too Low	The Offer A Raise Perks & Bennies	_____ _____ _____
Just Right	A Review	_____

Figure 6-1. Summary Chart for They Go First
—The Outcomes

Chapter 7
Salary-Making Rule 5:
Clinch The Deal, Then Deal Some More

Negotiating Bennies and Perks

Sometime during your post-offer silence your interviewer might say, "Now that might seem low, but keep in mind our liberal benefits program: free beer at the company picnic, your own space in the parking lot, a half day off at Christmas and a full-page spread in the company newsletter." Don't let these incredible goodies distract you from your first priority, your take-home pay. First come to an agreement on things like salary, commissions, and bonuses. Then move on to the bennies and perks.

"Bennies" is slang for benefits, "perks" for hiring perquisites. They are important for two reasons. First, they can complement a solid salary, making the total package even better. Second, if the salary you've been offered isn't quite what you expected, adding on some of these often-nontaxable extras can bring the entire offer very close to the figure you had in mind. That is the meaning of Salary-Making Rule 5: *Clinch the deal, then deal some more.*

Study the following eight subsections, which cover examples of typical bennies and perks you may wish to negotiate. You might choose not to discuss all of them at your first negotiating session. Bring up a few of the major ones and save the others for a second session. Don't worry if you can't resolve all of them right away, either. Some may be new to your employers, and they may need a few days to see what's possible.

After considering bennies and perks, we'll see why it's vital to take time to think it over, how to juggle two or more offers, and when to get an offer in writing.

Salary Reviews

The first thing to explore after negotiating your base salary is the salary review. One of the reasons for negotiating the best base salary first is that raises are generally computed as a percentage on that base. The higher the base, the greater the 2-, 3-, or 10-percent raise will be.

In negotiating a review there are three areas to consider: timing, basis, and percentage. Although you can't come up with the actual percentage now (if you could there would be no need for a review later on), you can influence it by taking a look at the cost-of-living adjustment (COLA).

The COLA is an automatic raise in salary to compensate for inflation. If your raise is 10 percent one year, but inflation 10 percent over the same time, then you haven't received a raise at all. You're simply being paid in purchasing power exactly what you earned the previous year. So you can bring up the subject of a review by talking about COLA.

You might say, "I expect that my salary will keep pace with inflation, so there will be a cost-of-living adjustment each year, won't there?" Once you get your potential employer to agree to a COLA, then you have already raised the actual percentage of your next raise because it will need to be computed and then added to the COLA. The government publishes several cost-of-living-adjustment indicators. The personnel department should be able to choose an appropriate one.

If you haven't got the base salary to the level that's acceptable to you, you might postpone discussion of the COLA and discuss the review process itself as a way to increase your salary. You might suggest that the employer hire you at the salary level you would like and then review your performance after six months to come up with a salary that feels fair. If that doesn't work, suggest that you split the difference. Try it for six months and go from there. Or you can start at the salary level you've been offered and negotiate for a review of your performance in six months. You might request a retroactive raise for that period, based on your performance.

Eli Djeddah, an early pioneer in job career consulting, suggests that you bring up the question of a review this way: "While my starting salary is important, I am also very interested in the future, since I expect to work here quite a while. In six months, when we review my performance, will it be on my demonstrated worth, or just a mechanical procedure?" Your employer will certainly choose the former, Eli asserts.

The timing of the review depends on you. Whatever time you estimate you will need to show tangible results, double it to be safe, and ask for the review at the end of that time. You can suggest that during your first week on the job you or your employer come up with a specific set of objectives that will be the basis for a review. That will demonstrate your conviction that salary should be the direct reflection of your contribution, not pie in the sky.

When you ask for a review in six months or any period shorter than a year, you may get objections concerning "company policy." Request a special exception because of your intention to really shine. You can say, "If we look at my performance in six months and I have not reached my objectives, it won't cost you a penny. If I do reach them, you will have made more than I cost, anyway. Either way, you win and I am motivated."

Sales Compensation

The next items to consider are commission rates or bonuses that you can earn. If you are in sales, you typically earn commissions. You can try to negotiate higher commission rates if you wish. If those are standardized and nonnegotiable, try asking for a higher commission rate over a certain quota. For example, if normal sales commissions are, say, 5 percent, you can ask that sales over $50,000 be paid a 6-percent commission.

Sales-compensation packages have several variations:

- straight commission,
- variable commission,
- draw against commission,
- advance against commission,
- base plus commission,
- salary plus commission,
- salary and bonus,
- salary, and
- residuals.

I will define them here and discuss the rationale behind each package.

Straight Commission: The commission phobia of some salespeople puzzles me. They want security; they confuse security with salary. On straight commission, your compensation is strictly a percentage of your sales. To many people that arrangement seems like the most risky, but it's actually the one most under your control. If you sell well, you're safe; no one will fire you. If you sell great, you're not only secure, you can practically write your own ticket.

Sometimes I wonder where they think a company's money comes from. Draws and advances are not gifts; they come out of your sales. They simply represent payment ahead of time of a portion of your future earnings. If you don't sell, you're no more secure on salary than on commission.

The best salespeople love straight commission because they know they get every dollar that's coming to them and that their income is entirely in their control. However, straight commission is not practical if you can't make sales right away. When the sales cycle is lengthy, straight commission is generally not workable.

Variable Commission: Same as straight commission, but the rate goes up or down depending on sales circumstances. You might be paid a higher commission on new accounts, on larger sales, or on total volume over a certain amount. Negotiating an increase in commission rate for top performance can be very lucrative and motivating.

Draw against Commission: Also straight commission, except the employer lets you draw a certain amount of money each pay period to help you get started. So if you have a $1,000 draw and you make only $800 in commissions, you would get a check for $1,000 and pay the company $200 back out of future earnings. Most draws are "forgivable," which means that if the job isn't working out you could quit and not have to pay back any money you owed the company. Do check this out.

Draws may last indefinitely or for a specified number of weeks or months, and the draw itself may be reduced or increased over time.

Advance against Commission: Like a draw, but it is generally an occasional, rather than a continual, event. It usually will not exceed the amount of commissions already earned.

Base plus Commission: Same as salary plus commission. Here the company pays you a certain salary, called your base. That's yours to keep and rely on. Above that, the company gives you a commission according to a mutually agreed-upon formula.

Salary: Some sales jobs pay a straight salary. These jobs almost always come with bonuses. If not, you can try to negotiate one.

Salary and Bonus: A bonus is a one-time payment of a fixed amount of money for achieving a certain volume of sales. It could be a weekly, monthly, quarterly, or even annual bonus or a bonus that automatically kicks in when you reach your goal.

Residual Commission: This is a type of commission that keeps on paying even if you quit the company. In insurance sales, for instance, after you've been with the company for a certain length of time, you're entitled, for a period of time, to a commission on the payments clients make to the policies you sold them whether or not you work for the company any longer.

When your sales work involves a lot of new-account generation, you would be wise to negotiate a residual commission on those new accounts. The justification here is that the reward for *selling* the account belongs to you; after you leave and the account is *maintained,* a portion of the income should still be yours for a while. Negotiate both the commission rate and the duration.

Watch out! Don't get cheated out of your commissions when you leave. One of the most common, but avoidable, misfortunes in negotiating sales commissions is not being clear about what happens when you leave the company.

Whatever your commission structure is, make sure you get clear exactly how commissions and pay are handled when you leave the company.

What sales do you get paid on, and when is the payment due? Often, commissions are payable when the client pays, not when the client is billed. Those payments may lag several months after the sale is made. Get it in writing now, when you begin. You don't want to fight this battle when you're gone; you'd lose. See the "Negotiating a Severance Package" sections in Chapter 8 for more about this.

Sales-Compensation Example

Here's an interesting example of negotiating commission compensation.

A client of mine moved into the art-sales field. She found a collection of valuable art that was being held in trust and was being stored for future sales. She wanted to be the agent to sell the paintings and didn't know how much to ask for in salary.

This example is very illustrative of the Make me a buck principle. Each party could make money for the other. The paintings were a cost to the estate while in storage; with the addition of Liz, they changed into a profit. Similarly, Liz without an art collection to market was just another Girl Friday. Both parties could win here. Now the question was who would win how much?

First, we determined her value in the matter. We figured that the collection as is would sell for $200,000 to a big gallery. By arranging special exhibits, auctions, and gallery showings, she estimated she could bring in $500,000 over time. Therefore, the difference between present and future sales would be $300,000, the "value added" she could produce. Whether it took her two years or twenty to do that, the added value to be shared in some fashion between her and the estate would still be $300,000.

However, the $300,000 was just an estimate (wild guess?). Who would bear the burden of the risk that the whole venture might be a flop? If she were on straight commission, taking on all the risks of the venture, she could negotiate for 50 to 85 percent of the net increased value (that's $150,000 to $240,000, about 30 to 50 percent of the estimated gross sales price); if she took all the risk, she ought to get most of the reward. On the other hand, if the estate would pay her living expenses for six months, perhaps the compensation would be base plus a smaller commission.

Paintings increase in value as their artists become better known. If Liz got the paintings into the hands of collectors, her work would be the ultimate reason for the increased value whether or not she was still actively marketing the works. Therefore, she could credibly negotiate for some residual commission on all works sold after she left.

Compensation could also be structured as commission or as a draw against commission. Since her risk is higher on commission, her reward should be higher than on a base or salary. If she earned a forgivable draw against commission, her risk would be less, so her commission might be less. On the other hand, if the estate wanted to take on all the risk, it could pay her a good salary for a year or two and call it even. She could also negotiate a salary with a bonus for a certain number of paintings sold within the first year.

Then she could lay claim to some of the more elusive dollars: the increased-earnings' interest as it builds over two, three, or more years and the savings generated as the storage costs decline. (Storing a painting is not like renting a U-Haul self-storage locker; it's big-buck climate control and high security.) On the other hand, taxes and the costs of transportation, gallery rental, and agent commission should be figured into the deal if it is to be fair.

So you can see how compensation can be arranged in many different ways, depending on what risk-reward ratio you're willing to accept. Notice that you can significantly increase your total compensation package by changing or adding *one element*.

Performance Bonuses

Even if you're not in sales, negotiating a performance bonus can be a very win-win way of earning extra income. A bonus based on the profitability of the area you're working in gives you an incentive to work and your employer a way to make more money. Retail-store managers, franchise operators, and department managers regularly get incentive bonuses based on target sales figures.

You can negotiate your own version of that no matter what your job. Just pin a number to the quantity or quality of your work using objectively measurable criteria. Or pose an open-ended question to your employer, like: "Let's consider setting up a special bonus to encourage excellent performance. Can you think of a workable one?"

Two variations of the bonus are profit sharing and stock options. Stock options used to be offered only to executives and the highest levels of corporate management. That makes sense, because their decisions directly affect the value of their company in the marketplace, and that value determines the price of the company's stock.

Recently, though, stock options have become available to lower levels of management. McDonald's stock options made Ray Kroc's secretary a millionaire. Some of the most motivating and successful companies have what are known as employee stock-ownership programs (ESOPs). See Chapter 9 for detailed information on negotiating stock options.

Although you would hardly be able to negotiate an entire ESOP for the company, you can suggest profit sharing if your work has a very direct bearing on the company's profits. Profit sharing can be computed monthly, quarterly, or annually as a percentage of the organization's gross or net revenues. Your research comes into play here, giving you a sense of what's standard for the particular field and the level of the position you're exploring.

Insurance

One benefit most companies offer is health insurance. Insurance plans vary from company to company, and you should ask to see what the plan and the coverage are. You may wish to negotiate for a different deductible in your medical program. You can also ask about dental insurance, life insurance, and special medical-expense provisions like disability pay. If you are unemployed and currently paying your own insurance premiums, you may negotiate to be covered right away by insurance rather than after the typical three-month waiting period.

While you're at it, double check that the insurance you do get from the company will extend three months beyond your termination date in the event you should leave. Some states have legislation requiring six months' post-employment medical coverage.

Legislation called COBRA (Consolidated Omnibus Budget and Reconciliation Act [of 1985]) requires that you be allowed, at your own expense, to remain on company health insurance at 101 percent of premium for up to a year or thirteen months after you leave. If you would like your employer to pay for X months of coverage when you leave, ask for it now.

Cars and Expense Accounts

For positions in which there is a lot of travel involved, discuss the travel-and-mileage allowance or the possibility of getting a company car. A company car may be worth several thousand dollars because it saves your paying insurance and maintenance costs on your own vehicle and depreciating that vehicle, and in certain cases may even save you all the taxes on those expenses.

In some tax situations, the benefits of an office in your home and other travel and expense reimbursements can make a tidy sum. Add it up: 27 percent (or more), income tax; 10 percent, FICA; 1 to 5 percent, state income tax—almost forty-five cents on the dollar! It's a lot easier to get a nontaxable monthly repayment for car, insurance, phone, travel, etc., than to save all those receipts and itemize them on April 15th. And your employer saves 8 percent in FICA contribution, too. Remember, you'll ultimately need documentation if the IRS asks for it. Check with your accountant; check with your employer's accountant; then solicit the opinion that favors you.

Another benefit to clear up now is the expense account or entertainment account, especially if you are in sales. What does the company consider customary expenses, and what exceptions are there?

Professional Memberships

If you have done your research for the position, you are probably aware of the professional association in your area of expertise. If you explain to the employer how a membership can help you be more productive for them, the employer should be willing to pay your membership dues and give you time off for meetings or training in your field.

Vacation and Personal Days

If you can't increase the money, perhaps you can reduce the time! Negotiate vacation, personal days, or your hours per week.

Let's get one thing clear on the vacation issue. No one pays you to go on vacation. You earn it. First, you earn it by doing extra work to help cover for others when they go on vacation. Second, you are paid only to bring in more money than you cost. You do not bring in money on vacation. So two weeks' vacation pay is really just fifty weeks of earnings spread out over fifty-two weeks. However, on vacation you do restore and replenish your energy (in theory, at least). Since that fresh energy can generate more profit, employers can sometimes be convinced that extra vacation bennies will pay off for them.

First, ask what the company's vacation, sick-day, and personal-day policies are. Then, when you discuss vacation, always frame it as a way to help you be more productive on the job. You might say, "I tend to throw myself so entirely into my work that I need a few breaks during the year to recharge; I'd like X weeks' vacation."

See if you can get at least one more week than they offer, even if it's five personal days scattered throughout the year. Or see if you can earn more vacation time or personal days by achieving 100-percent attendance over a given period of time. Many companies would prefer that their employees call in well and take prearranged, earned wellness days rather than call in sick on short notice.

Relocation Expenses

Relocation expenses aren't always offered. They are generally part of a new compensation package whenever your *present* employer requests that you relocate. With a new employer, it is common only in executive positions, or whenever the employer wants you badly enough.

Some relocation perks that you can calculate and might consider requesting are company purchase of your present or future home and company payments of moving fees, closing costs, real-estate-broker's fees, any early-mortgage-prepayment penalty, mortgage-rate differentials, your family's transportation costs of looking at new homes, appliance installation, and lodging fees while looking at or waiting for a new home.

Other Bennies and Perks

Here's a list of some other things you might consider: severance pay; Christmas bonuses; matching-funds investment program; deferred salary; corporate gasoline from private pumps; free parking; corporate cafeteria or executive-dining-room privileges; pension plans (do you contribute or does the company pay in full?); credit union; company-paid physical examinations; country-club or health-club memberships; and use of the corporate plane, boat, or vacation property. With so many takeovers, downsizing, etc., negotiating severance pay can be very important. See the Special Situations chapter to learn more, especially the section, "Negotiating Severance Timing II: Long before you need it."

Also ask about tuition reimbursement. Are there specific courses or degree work that would help you perform your job? Ask if the company will pay, or help pay, some of those costs.

Still more bennies and perks are estate- or financial-planning assistance, tax and legal assistance, and corporate-product discounts. Figure 7-1 contains a list of perquisites and benefits.

Signing Bonus (a.k.a. "Sign-On" Bonus)

In flush times generally, or when demand is high in your particular specialty, employers may entice you to take their offer by adding a signing bonus. This is a one-time multi-thousand dollar payment and its purpose can be to…

- sweeten the offer so you'll take it;

- compensate you for bonuses, options vesting, etc., you would lose with your present company if you accept the offer from the new one (they "make you whole.");

- recognize the IV$ value you bring (i.e. you're saving them $5,000 tuition in, say, Peachtree software because you already know it.);

- reward you for bringing over your "book" of business or your loyal-to-you clients.

Any time you can think of special IV$ (see chapter 4), you have a rationale for negotiating this type of bonus.

Time to Think It Over

After you've discussed these matters, the offer should be pretty clear. You've worked hard, held your ground, and believed in yourself. Now comes the hard part: DON'T TAKE THE JOB! (Yet.)

I. BASIC COMPENSATION

Base salary, Sales commission, Bonuses, Signing bonus

II. BENEFITS

Vacation time, Sick days, Wellness days, COLA

Insurance: Life, Medical, Dental, Disability

III. PERQUISITES

Profit sharing	Financial-planning assistance
Stock options	Pension plan
Legal assistance	Child care
Tuition reimbursement	Country-club membership
Special training courses	Luncheon-club membership
Deferred compensation	Athletic-club membership
C.P.A. and tax assistance	Consumer-product discounts
Executive-dining-room privileges	Company car or travel allowance
Matching-investment program 401K	Professional/trade-association dues

IV. RELOCATION

Moving expenses, Closing costs, Mortgage-rate differential.

Mortgage-prepayment penalty, Real-estate brokerage fees.

Trips for your family to look for a home.

Lodging fees while between homes .

Shipping of boats and pets.

Installation of appliances, drapes, and carpets.

V. MISCELLANEOUS

Annual physical exam; Special training courses; Mortgage funds/loans.

Severance pay, Starting date, Future salary reviews.

Office space, equipment, Secretarial and support staff.

Outplacement assistance upon termination.

Overrides on others' performance.

Time & costs of trade shows, professional conferences.

Figure 7-1. Base, Bennies and Perks Checklist

Money decisions are best made in the cool climate of logic and impartiality. Remember, you've been working toward this offer for months! You're eager and stimulated. It's new and exciting. But deciding in the heat of the moment makes for poor financial decisions. Anyone who's compared a grocery bill run up while shopping hungry with one while shopping with a full stomach would concur.

Give yourself time to think, but don't be cool, indifferent, or undecided. When you've finished negotiating, put all your enthusiasm back in gear and say, "This sounds terrific! I think we've really got a solid match here. Would you jot this all down so we're clear? and I'll get back to you *as soon as you need to know.* When *do* you need to know?"

It is extremely important to maintain your enthusiastic voice, gestures, and energy so your request for time is not taken as a lack of interest in the job. There's a delicate line here between demanding time and requesting clarity.

Don't Be "Cool"

One client lost an offer because, instead of framing a delay as a request for clarity, he made it a demand: "I'll need time to think about this. I'll call you in a couple of days." "Well," the employer responded—they had been talking for weeks—"if you're still undecided, we don't want you." The employer had interpreted his "think about this" response as lack of commitment or enthusiasm.

Put yourself in Ms. Employer's shoes. She has concluded a long, arduous process of finding the person who is finally going to solve her problems. She has struggled through nebulous and difficult negotiations with you and struck a deal. She is now eager to close the deal and the last thing she wants to hear is, "I'll think about it" (especially since, as any salesperson can tell you, "I'll think it over" is usually a polite way of saying no). On the other hand, you do need some time to make sure all the bases are covered.

How to Enthusiastically Ask for Time to Think It Over

How do you ask for it? Here are some more examples: "Yes! We're done! I can't wait to get started. I will need to look this over to make sure we haven't forgotten anything, so when do you want my final confirmation?" Or: "Okay, I'm giving my tentative yes right now and I'll give you the permanent one as soon as you need to hear it. When would that be?" [Answer.] "Okay, I don't see anything left to talk about right now. I'll sleep on this, look at it again to make sure we haven't missed anything, and confirm it in writing by that date."

Juggling Two or More Offers

What if you can't operate on the company's timetable? Suppose the company wants a decision in one week and you have another offer pending that will take two weeks to mature? Then it's best to suggest your own time frame and see if the company can work within it.

"This meets all my criteria for what I want," you say, "and I have every indication that this is the correct match, but I want to consider this very carefully. I'd like two weeks to let this decision settle. Will that work with your schedule?"

Sometimes it will, sometimes it won't. The hardest part about job hunting is that offers generally come one at a time. You are seldom comparing one offer with another. Instead you're comparing a bird in the hand with two in the bush. The key in buying time to leverage other offers is to concentrate not so much on getting the firm offer extended as on accelerating the pending one.

If your pending offer has any strength at all, then you have a good relationship established already with the hiring individual (generally not the same as the personnel person). Use that rapport. You will need to have a face-to-face meeting with this potential boss, explain the problem, and ask for assistance in solving it.

Figure 7-2. Juggling Two or More Offers

"I have another offer," you explain. "The job is not better than yours, or worse, just different. Frankly, my preference is to take the one in which I can make the best contribution. How can we get things moving here to meet the deadline of the first offer?"

If you have good rapport, you can work together to accelerate things. If there's no interest in assisting you, that's a strong indication that the second offer is less of a fit than the first.

Sometimes, however, job two (pending) can't be hurried and job one (firm) can't be delayed. So if you're pressed to give a yes or no to job one without having a yea or nay from employer two, use your own judgment. You can:

- Tell job one about job two and press for more time: "The reason I'd like that extra week is to get all the facts about another pending offer. Can we arrange it?"

- Tell job one yes, but warn the people there that, if job two comes up, you would have to consider accepting it and quitting theirs.

- Tell job one yes and cross the next bridge if you come to it. (You should be able to find a way to compensate employer one fairly for the month of training and the cost of hiring a replacement if you later pick job two. If that is not your plan, then this is not good human relations, and will probably come back to haunt you.)

- Tell job one yes and forget job two.

Probably the best way to make the choice is to use your own internal measurement of which job would work best. Tell that one yes. Period. Even if it means losing the bird in the hand *and* the two in the bush. Your integrity and focus will soon line up job four, which may be better than all its predecessors.

How do you decide which is best?

Examine the offers and grade each of them A through F in these areas: satisfaction, professional growth, growth in responsibility, location, people and company style, and compensation. Those are explained in Figure 7-3. Fill in the chart by writing down the grades and then numbering each area in order of importance: priority 1 through 6.

PRIORITY		GRADE	
		JOB 1	JOB 2
Satisfaction Opportunity to be doing work activities in which I am skilled in and enjoy.			
Professional Growth Opportunity to expand my skills and become a better professional in my field			
Growth in Responsibility Opportunity to be promoted, or to expand the job to take on higher-level problems as I master the present ones.			
Location Commuting distance and geographical location of the job. Amount of travel required			
People/Company Style Are they people I can work with? Is the company managed in a style that will allow me to be successful?			
Compensation Wages, bennies, perks.			

Figure 7-3. Offer Comparison Chart

Start with your highest priority, and compare the jobs point by point; you'll know which is the better offer.

If it's still too close to tell, then what are you waiting for? Tell job one yes and job two no!

Counter-Offers

Occasionally, juggling two offers will stem from a surprise: a counteroffer from your present company. There is no absolute right or wrong thing to do about a counteroffer, but there are important considerations. Consider first an objective comparison using the format described above. If the counteroffer is better than the market offer, then consider whether the real reasons you wanted to leave your present company are still valid. If there is concrete evidence that those reasons have been handled, you can accept the counteroffer.

Usually, however, breaking the news that you want another job will leave a sour taste in your present employer's mouth. They are in shock and they make an instinctive play to retain you. Without *prior* evidence that real changes are being made, all their promises about things being better from now on are, as Mary Poppins would say, "Pie-crust promises: easily made, easily broken."

Urgent Employers

Occasionally your prospective employer will ask you to decide right in the room. Whether you are juggling many offers or desperately clinging to one, you do not want to do that.

You've said, "I'll get back to you as soon as you need to know. When *do* you need to know?"

You're told, "We need to have your answer right now."

You ask for clarification: "Fine, tell me about that."

You're told, "Charlie's flying to London, Sharon's going on vacation, and we need someone aboard by Monday. We need to know right now."

That seems reasonable, so you work with it.

If you're at all interested, say, "Yes! This looks great! Right now I'm ready to accept, but I like to make my decisions carefully. I'm sure you would want careful decisions from me when I'm working for you. I can't see that anything would come up to change my mind but, if there's any way to get me some objective time to solidify my thinking on this, I would appreciate it." If an impulsive decision is wanted, you'll oblige. Say yes and base it on your judgment of the moment. If something comes up before Monday, you'll call back and (impulsively) say no!

In any event, leave the negotiations open a little: "Decide now? Why, yes, of course! I accept! There may be a detail or two in the compensation package we've overlooked, so if I think of anything I'll let you know in the next couple of days."

Now remember something presented in the "Time to Think It Over" section: "Would you jot this all down?"

When to Get It in Writing

There's four levels of getting it in writing:

Level 1.   "jotting it down" so we're clear,

Level 2.   getting a written formal offer from the company,

Level 3.   extra contractual agreements like non-compete, non-disclosure, non-solicitation, and confidentiality, and

Level 4.   unique features of your employment or compensation that limit an employer's right to fire you "at will."

Level 1 applies every time. In hurry-up situations it's doubly important to get it "jotted down" before you leave the negotiating table. Things are going fast and you want to know that what you bargained for will not get lost in the shuffle. Putting it in writing is a way of getting your employer to be extra awake, aware and clear about the terms, dates, amounts, etc. I recommend the word "jot." "Let's jot it down so we're clear" is more user-friendly and less intimidating than "Let's write it up."

If the company policy is to send a written/e-mailed offer letter, that's Level 2. As long as you have agreed to a definite date for acceptance, there should be no danger of losing an offer to interlopers and you can wait for a confirmation letter from the employer. Especially when the offer is more complicated than the standard one of salary, benefits, and starting date, "jot it down."

If you want a little more control of the situation, you can offer to write and send a letter of acceptance that reiterates the offer. Compose that letter from the notes you "jotted down" at the time.

Write up the elements of the offer neatly during the interview and ask your employer to look it over. Then have a duplicate made for yourself. You'll be glad you got it all clear and so will your employer.

Level 3. Sometimes employers have non-compete, non-disclosure, etc., agreements for you to sign. They may look like innocent boilerplate documents, but don't sign them yet. Read about these in Special Situations, Chapter 8.

Level 4 occurs when you have a lot at stake by accepting an offer—as when having to resign another position. You may want to limit the employer's right to hire/fire "at will." You'll definitely want the offer in writing, and this time it should be typed out in a formal letter, and you may need a contract prepared by a lawyer. Generally you'll have no problem getting that letter and, more important, a day to solidify your decision. Situations requiring a formal contract are also covered in Chapter 8 under "When Do I Need to Talk to a Lawyer."

Delay giving notice to your present employer until you have your letter or formal agreement from the new one.

Final Acceptance of an Offer

The final acceptance of an offer can be done by phone. In the normal-paced version of this option, you will take the time you need to think through the offer coolly before calling to accept.

When you call, you may request a more formal written offer so that you don't quit your present job, then find yourself unemployed. In larger companies the personnel department provides one within a week. Or you can offer to write a detailed letter of acceptance yourself, if you wish. In any event, communicate your enthusiasm once again, and assure your employer how well you expect this to work out.

What if I Like it Now—Can I Just Say "Yes"?

What if you know the job is perfect and the package is super? Why *not* say yes right away? Well, besides depriving yourself of the objectivity you'd gain by waiting, it's a matter of style. As Eli Djeddah, a pioneer in career counseling, has said, "It's simply not dignified." You want to be treated with respect when you begin your new job. If you wait before accepting the offer, you'll be respected for your clear-headed approach to things, and your employer's joy with its new-found employee will be all the more sweet for its day or so of pacing in the waiting room.

Chapter 8
Special Situations

This chapter deals with some situations job seekers often encounter in their campaigns. These situations may require special strategies or, in some cases, making exceptions to the salary-making rules. The chapter also includes a *special consideration*: how to present a good image to employers.

Ads and Applications with "Salary History Required"

Some ads get pretty nosy about your salary requirements. However, even an ad that reads:

Salary history required. Résumés without salary histories will be shredded into oblivion and each applicant excommunicated ipso facto, held up to public scorn and opprobrium, fined, imprisoned, and in various and sundry ways maltreated...

should end

...and hired if we think you can help us out of our mess.

Want ads have been described as "desperate screams for help emanating from somewhere deep in the corporate diaphragm." They are last resorts from people who need help so badly they are willing to pay to advertise, then sift through hundreds of résumés. I don't care how strongly an ad demands your numbers, employers will not pass you over if you're right for the job, *provided you show them respect.*

Why do employers want these figures?   To screen, remember? They don't want to waste the time talking to you if they can't "afford" you in their budget stage. Your best approach to their ads is to acknowledge their need to screen, then stick to your principles about postponing money until there's a match.

So in your cover letter write something like: "I understand you've requested a salary history. I'm paid roughly the market value of a [job title] with X years' experience and, though I'm not willing to publish my compensation package, I'd be happy to discuss it in an interview. I don't think salary will be a problem." Then in the interview say, "The amount of responsibility looks right, here, and since I'd be interested in fitting into your salary structure I'm sure we can come to a good agreement.   Let's discuss the job and the match for the moment."

Internet boxes "Enter Salary History Here"

When you apply online, you often run into a box that will not let you leave it empty. I do not advise putting "0" [zero] there because it can look smart-alecky. On the other hand, you don't want to be screened out, either and you'll never get to the "submit" button unless you enter something. So, I suggest you do some good ORV$ research (Chapter 5) and put a number there that conveys the message: "I am a good candidate, not too expensive and not too cheap."

The same message applies to a paper application form, but there, when it asks for salary expectations, you can write "Open."

When it asks for previous salary history, leave it blank.

If it says, "Fill in every blank and answer every question," put "Competitive" with an asterisk in the salary slot and a note at the bottom saying, "*I'd be glad to discuss this personally in an interview." In the interview say, "I'd be glad to discuss it in a *hiring* interview. I don't think salary will be a problem. Let's see how I can help you."

Discussing Salary at Networking Interviews

During job interviews always follow Salary-Making Rule 1: *Postpone salary discussions until you have been offered the job.* However, during information-gathering interviews, salary discussions can sometimes be appropriate. Occasionally, people will want to know your salary expectations as a way of understanding what level of work you want and are able to handle.

I instructed one client of mine to *begin* her networking interviews with a salary discussion. Since she was working for a temporary-services agency, she could be mistaken for an eight-dollar-an-hour gofer unless she made her potential clear. She started her conversations with a statement like: "I know I'm able to handle responsibilities that pay in the high thirties. I'm flexible about where I start and I'm interested in talking with you to identify paths to that end."

That brings up the question of how to ask for salary information when you're *not* interviewing for a job.

In the United States, discussing one's salary is practically taboo in social conversation. People are curious about who's making what, but are too afraid to ask. So when you offer a you-tell-me-yours-and-I'll-tell-you-mine deal, it's too good to pass up. Even then you'll be getting only a range, with their salaries situated anonymously in the middle.

People often attach identity, status, value, and prestige to their incomes, so revealing them can be scary, too intimate. I know counselors, lawyers, mechanics, and even baby sitters who are too shy to ask peers what they charge per hour. Nevertheless, if you intend to add a networking approach to your job-hunting campaign, you'll need to discuss salary with your contacts. It will probably feel awkward to discuss it and awkward to avoid it, but you need to discuss it.

Keep in mind again that your salary is linked to your level of responsibility. You need to treat salary as a thermometer; you'll be telling people how much heat you can take. Before you seriously talk to people on your job hunt, do the research as described in Chapter 5. Look at the jobs and ask yourself which one you realistically think you could best handle. Get the range by looking it up. Then do a reality check on your expectations by discussing your findings on information-gathering interviews.

Phrasing your check on responsibilities you can handle might sound like: "What are the biggest challenges you could see me handling? And what do positions like that pay?"

Another research question you can ask a contact is: "With the amount of experience you see in me, and considering the functions I can handle, what would you estimate my salary range in this field to be?" And you can follow up with: "Well, I've researched [supervisor] positions in the [travel] industry, [production-supervisor] positions in [light manufacturing], and a few other types of positions, and I come up with a range of X to Y dollars. What would I have to do in your field to get that kind of money?"

You can, if you like, go first in such a situation. As long as you aren't discussing a specific job opening, it figures to be an open-ended conversation that's not likely to box you in. That's especially true if you're talking about your researched estimate. Remember, too, that interviewers may not really know how to answer you.

You probably realize by now that, since people would sooner discuss their sex lives and last sessions with their therapist than reveal their salaries, others' estimates of your earning abilities may really be a blind guess. Your own estimates may educate *them* on the size of the problems you want to handle. With that clarity, you'll get better-quality referrals to other contacts.

Special Considerations: Image and Communication

Part of getting top dollar is your self-presentation. If your own estimate of value and competence is not matched by your contacts' estimates, the problem could be your image or communication.

Image. Getting what you're worth through your image requires dressing in your salary range, displaying etiquette in your salary range, grooming in your salary range, and speaking in your salary range. There are studies that show the most reliable indicator of a person's salary level is vocabulary, and that a limp, fishy handshake could cost you thousands of dollars.

Look around you and notice the way your target-level people dress and act. Imitate them or their superiors. A client of mine heeded my advice and dressed in a well-fitting, moderately priced suit when the position he was interviewing for was very "short sleeves." The business owner who interviewed him said he was overqualified for that position, but had been thinking of another position more in his line. Investment: one $350 suit; return: twelve hundred percent—one job $5,000 better than the original.

Communication. Besides looking the part, you also need to communicate your capabilities in a strong, positive way that is directly understandable and applicable to your prospective employer's needs. It's common sense that the stronger you construct the match and compatibility, the more **fudgit** and **judgit** you'll engender.

Being a job and career consultant, I of course recommend *minimally* consulting a candid friend for a critique of your self-presentation. And if you *really* want the best return from your efforts, hire a coach, a career consultant whose reputation you've researched. Besides saving you time (which equals money) in your job hunt and focusing you on your best market possibilities, a coach can really train you to sell yourself at the top of your potential.

"Overqualified"

The well-dressed client above evoked a constructive "Overqualified" response. But what if "Overqualified" is negative? I had a less-fortunate client who applied for two almost-identical positions in two very similar companies. One told him he couldn't handle the job, the other that he was overqualified, a very subjective term that can mean different things.

"Overqualified" relates to salary negotiations one time out of three. It means your potential employer is worried that 1) you'll be bored, so bored that you'll last a few months, then quit for more exciting work; 2) you'll be expensive, so expensive that you'll work a few months, then quit for a better-paying job; 3) you're a creep, such a creep that in a few days you'll alienate everybody and get fired.

The first is a focus issue; the second, a salary issue; the third — well, in Fritz Perls' words: "If by chance we find each other, it's beautiful. If not, it can't be helped."

The first means the job isn't really for you. Unless you're interested in starting in the cellar and working your way up, you should refocus the interview on where the company might have challenges at your level.

The second is a situation covered by Salary-Making Rule 1. If you're being judged as too expensive, then salary has become an issue even though you haven't explicitly discussed it, in which case you're really discussing salary before the offer. Although it's still too early to discuss numbers, you should bring up and face this issue head on.

A variation of "I'm sure we can come up with a good salary agreement" works well. Or try: "Overqualified? I'm glad you brought that up, because I want a job that will work out well for a *long time*. So far this seems like the right kind of challenge for me. If salary is an issue, I'm sure we can handle that if the job is right." Or simply: "Overqualified? Maybe you're worrying that you can't pay me enough and I'd leave. Don't. If the job is right and the money is fair, I'll be satisfied."

Again, you must know yourself and the job well enough. If it really is below your capabilities and you see no potential to expand the duties, then you *are* overqualified and shouldn't be interviewing for that position in the first place.

Exceptions: Recruiters and Employment Agencies

What if you register with employment agencies (which place support staff) or recruiters (who work with higher-level professionals and executives)? What do you tell them when they ask about salary?

I am revising my second-edition advice.

In that edition, I said that both types of intermediaries are exceptions. I advocated total candor and said you *may* discuss salary expectations first. I asserted that such intermediaries, to screen you, legitimately needed to know your salary requirements. I explained that the purpose of postponing salary discussion is to give yourself time to move the employer from **budget** to **fudgit** to **judgit** and that when you're dealing with an intermediary you're within the **budget** stage, only. I said so because, at least initially, only the intermediary has contact with the employer. So since you won't get to the **fudgit** or **judgit** stages if you withhold salary, I recommended that, when dealing with recruiters, you let them know your current earnings and requirements, especially the salary that represents the amount of challenge you can handle.

I said the same goes concerning employment agencies. Instead of holding back your expectations, sometimes you'll have to be *doubly* clear about what salary you will and won't accept, or you'll be running all over town talking to people about low-paying jobs. (Throughout the rest of this section, I'll refer to the intermediary as the "recruiter" though the above principles hold true for employment agents as well.)

Since that edition, I have done telecoaching with several people who have not benefited by disclosing current earnings to a recruiter. So what should you do? Read the rest of this section. It contains my original advice and rationale with a few side comments where needed; then read the example that follows, where I will temper my original advice.

When asked about their current earnings, some people are tempted to inflate them. Never do that. There are three sound reasons why I recommend 100-percent truth in stating your salary information:

- Frank money talk with a recruiter shows integrity and good faith;

- Recruiters can often sense when you are fabricating your earnings, and they're trained in effective methods of getting at the truth, which include verifying with previous employers, a service their client, the employer, expects and is paying for;

- Experienced recruiters are excellent judges of value, so salary history will not prejudice them, and you can still establish your real value with facts about your performance potential. (Side comment: I've learned that only *some* recruiters will not be prejudiced by salary history; others will still use it as a measuring stick; proceed with caution.)

Even though you'll lack contact with the employer at the start, experienced recruiters are generally pretty accomplished, themselves, at moving an employer from **budget** to **judgit**. Since the fee they earn for a placement—believe me, they do earn it— usually depends on the first year's salary, they'll try to get you the highest offer possible. On the other hand, since they're paid only upon placement, just getting you hired is their first priority. Your salary is secondary. If the employer "can't afford you," the recruiter will look for another candidate. (Job-hunting tip: In such a case, ask the recruiter if there are other client companies who might want your talents. If you are a very strong candidate, some recruiters will market you to their client base to earn extra fees. Marketing a candidate, rather than filling a job order, is the exception, not the rule, but you've got nothing to lose!)

Paradoxically, recruiters' concern for just getting you hired, which can **budget** you out, can also motivate recruiters to bend the budget for you. Why? Because they want a compensation package attractive enough to make you say yes!

Recruiters usually at least try to extend the offer on the company's behalf. Before they present it, they make every effort to clear all aspects of it with the hiring person. That includes dollars, incentives, bennies, perks, relocating expenses, sign-on bonuses, and others. Sometimes recruiters negotiate the offer; sometimes, since they have no authority to spend their clients' money, this is precisely the time they bow out. Often, then, the candidate is able to negotiate the offer directly with the employer during the interview. You'll need only to know who actually is handling the negotiations in your case.

Will your recruiter spill the beans and hurt your negotiating position with the employer? Well, recruiters invariably tell the employer your current or past earnings when asked. However, if the candidate earns more than the budgeted salary, but the employer is able to go higher, the recruiter may withhold the candidate's earnings information until the employer has interviewed that person. I know a recruiter who got a candidate $30,000 more that way.

Often, however, the employer is firm about the highest potential offer. If that looks like a problem, the recruiter will, by asking the candidate if the range is okay, avoid putting any more time into what might be an unworkable situation. If that happens to you, you *may* choose to interview, anyway, especially if you're unemployed or the opportunity looks especially good.

However, you should know that an experienced recruiter won't send out on an interview candidates who

- are motivated to look at a new position because of money, only;

- won't reveal their earnings or are found to have exaggerated them;

- would entertain a counteroffer from their current employers;

- have unrealistic expectations about the salary or job they'll accept.

During your interview with the employer, Salary-Making Rule 1 remains in effect, though you here approach it differently. Your aim is still to establish value before discussing price. However, since, when asked, recruiters reveal your past or current earnings to their client companies—after all, the employer pays the fee—it doesn't matter if you, too, tell the employer. Your recruiter should actually suggest that you do. The recruiter should also show you how to sell your worth.

When the employer asks, "What salary are you looking for?" you can say, "I'm sure that, if you could double your current earnings with the right job, you'd jump at the chance, wouldn't you? So would I. But realistically, I'm earning X dollars now, and I hope that an offer will be somewhere between that and twice that figure, based on your recognition of my true worth to your organization." Or: "When the recruiter described your company and opportunity, she explained that your firm was very competitive and that you typically hire top talent as a result. That assures me that when you make me an offer it will be both fair and attractive."

Candidates who report their earnings to the dollar without prompting get high marks for honesty, and everything else they say about their backgrounds becomes easier to accept. So it's acceptable to go ahead and give both the recruiter and the employer your exact salary, but make it very clear what *range* you think you're qualified for. (Side comment: Read the following example. If you can get by without disclosing current earnings, you might come out ahead.)

Exceptions: Recruiters and Agencies—Revisions

A telecoaching client of mine concluded some negotiations that illustrate a difficulty here. Unfortunately, he didn't contact me until *after* he had made a blunder.

Many negotiation books suggest you inflate your current salary by tacking on your benefits, perks, and bonuses. Thus, if you're making, say, $75,000 and bonus, you tell the employer (or recruiter) you're making $95,000. My client, Tom (not his real name), did that and eventually got an offer from the Atlanta-based employer at $120,000 plus a relocation package, and bonuses.

Then he contacted me. He was worried that eventually his actual current salary would be disclosed, that somewhere down the line he'd find himself in a pickle because after leaving his present job he might be left out in the cold if the new company fired him for not having told the whole truth.

We did some calculations. If he played it right it was *unlikely*, say one chance in ten, that the "white lie" would ever really come to light. The risk-reward question was: Are you willing to take a 10-percent risk that it will all fall apart and your integrity will be questioned for the 90-percent chance that you'll make $45,000 more each year and have a great job with plenty of growth and challenge? The window for living with this uncertainty was one year. (We thought it extremely unlikely that anyone would ever uncover this after a year or, if someone did, would care by then, since Tom could always say, "Well my base was $75,000, but my *package* was around $95,000," anyway.)

Tom decided that living under the sword of Damocles for a year was a price he was not willing to pay. So we set about cleaning up the matter. He called the recruiter and said, "I am very interested in this offer, but I want to clarify something before we go further. First, tell me, do you think this $120,000 offer is a fair market value for the job, and for my talents in this situation?"

Recruiter, "Oh, yes [blah blah]."

Tom (to himself), "Gotcha!"

Tom, "Well, that's what I thought. It makes me want to clear up a misunderstanding we may have had earlier in our discussions. When you asked me, 'Where are you now?' I responded $95,000. You should know that that was the value of my entire compensation package, including projected year-end bonuses and benefits. My actual base salary is $75,000. If you think this discrepancy would have any adverse effect on the Atlanta company's offer, we should clear it up now."

Recruiter, "That's terrible! Why did you say that? Now I'm in a bind with the Atlanta company. That means they'd be giving you a 60-percent raise! They'll never go for that." He continued to vent for a while.

Mind you, this was a top recruiter from a high-end, well-respected, IBM-of-the-industry retained-search firm. He was – misguidedly, I think – basing the offer on *current earnings, not the freely agreed-upon market value!*

The short of it is that the company *did* rescind the offer. In my opinion, it was not because the dollar figure wasn't right but because the company insisted on people who could be absolutely trusted in those positions, so didn't want to start a relationship from a "Well, I lied" foundation.

End of story.

So what do we learn from this?

If Tom had held firm in the beginning he might have avoided that trap. He could have said, "I can't disclose my exact earnings now but, let me tell you, it's a lot! What's more important is my worth in a next move. I've researched the industry, and I think my next move should be to responsibilities paying anywhere between $110,000 and $175,000. That total package would be composed of a significant base and good performance incentives. The actual dollar number will depend on location—the colder the climate is, the more money I'll need—overall growth potential of the position, range of autonomy, visibility in the industry, benefits, perks, relocation package, signing bonus, and many other factors. Why don't we see if I like the job and, if they like me first; salary won't be an issue for the right job. What is the company?"

This response is honest, clear, based on research, and completely avoids current earnings. Will a recruiter buy it? Maybe; maybe not. It's worth a try.

Salary Boxes

Sometimes you'll be negotiating with a company that has compensation all figured out ahead of time. Perhaps it has implemented the Hay system, or the ranges have been set by law — public-sector positions are often confined so — and you fit into a category. Teaching positions are systematically boxed into academic degrees and years of experience. Each box has its own salary attached. The federal government has grades and steps within grades; positions are assigned a rating of G.S. 8, G.S. 9, and so on, and a standard salary.

You *can* negotiate these, though it's harder. If you can't change the salary attached to the box, perhaps you can change the box. Doesn't your volunteer work with Great Books and your adult-education class work really add up to another year of teaching experience? Perhaps your two years in that inner-city school is equivalent to three or four years of normal teaching. (It took several years off your life, that's for sure!)

The other strategy to use is reassigning the grade itself. The earlier in the formation stages a job is, the easier it is to do that. If the job has been classified as G.S. 5 for years and years, it's unlikely you can make a case for upgrading it, unless you can negotiate some added responsibilities to it. But if it's a new position, you might be able to show how it really should be upgraded.

A client of mine was told in the interviewing process that a particular company's policy was to give all the information about degree, experience, project assignment, and so forth to the personnel department, and it would come up with an offer. That was it! He could only take it or leave it once it was figured out! Sound nonnegotiable? Well, we found a way for him to make the right noises to the right ears about his value and about the importance of getting the compensation figured out attractively. Although we couldn't change the final number, we influenced beforehand the people who made up that number. When the offer came in, it was a 100-percent salary increase over his present job.

Phil's Salary-Boxes Story

Another client, Phil, interviewed to teach at a public high school. Three times during the interview the principal said, "You understand that this is an eight-tenths position, don't you?" (That meant it was a four-day-a-week job, so drew 80 percent of full-time salary.)

"Well," my client replied, "I understand that it's an eight-tenths position, and if I'm the one you want I'm sure we can find a way to work out fair compensation."

Turns out my client *was* the one they wanted, but eight-tenths of the salary box was too low for him to accept. So first he tried to get eight-tenths of a different box. Would the principal consider his master's degree the equivalent of "master's plus fifteen hours"? After all, it had required thirty more credit hours than other teachers' master's degrees.

"Sorry, no," the principal responded.

Then how about credit for an extra year of experience, since his master's internship had been a very demanding full-time position for six months with delinquent kids?

"No, any exceptions would bring on grievances from other teachers in the union."

Well, how about special assignments like debating coach, or computer & audio-visual equipment coordinator?

"Aha! We could explore that, yes! Ms. Smith, the chemistry teacher has just had a baby and might be interested in handing the equipment someone else."

Result: eight-tenths position plus a few hours' coordinating school equipment, equaling a total salary 10 percent *higher* than a *full-time* position in that box. Of further interest is that six people had interviewed for and *rejected* the position when they learned it was only eight-tenths. Phil scored!

The moral is that, when interviewers say "inflexible" or "nonnegotiable," they're still in the **budget** stage. So wait for **judgit**, and look for ways to change the box you fit in, the box the job fits in, or the box-makers' minds!

Over the Phone

Final acceptance of an offer can be handled by phone, but whenever possible avoid doing the initial negotiating that way. If you are given an offer over the phone, tell the individual that it sounds very workable and, since it is important that the agreement be clear and good for both parties, you'd like to stop in and talk it over in detail. You will have a better opportunity to get a fully negotiated deal when you and your potential employer are giving it your full attention, which you can't do on the phone.

When it's not possible to stop in, you can make sure you and the employer are undisturbed and able to negotiate as you would face to face by simply setting a time to call back to handle it. Otherwise, you're off guard or likely to be caught in the middle of something. Call back at a time when you can concentrate on negotiating.

Delayed Negotiations

Another special area to note is delayed salary discussions. You know from Salary-Making Rule 1 to wait for a job offer before discussing salary, but don't wait longer than that. If you get a hiring signal from an employer who doesn't bring up salary, *you* bring it up.

You could say, "Well, I guess that means we'd better make a deal. What did you have in mind?"

Letting it go beyond offer time could mean your employer plans to hire you without negotiating and assumes you'll take what you get. Or else the employer's embarrassed.

I had a client who had every indication that the director of engineering wanted to hire him. The director had said, "You're just the person we're looking for."

"What was their offer?" I asked.

"Oh, we haven't talked money yet."

Uh-oh!

He quickly followed my instructions to get right back on the phone, ask how firm the decision was, and suggest that they talk about salary. He was told, "Well, we'd love to have you, but you wouldn't take $58,000, would you?"

"Well, I'd consider it," he replied. "When can we talk, and who makes those decisions?"

He was hired two weeks later at a grade higher than the opening was originally rated at. He made an extra $7,500 a year because he'd negotiated for his market value and fuller responsibilities. If he had waited, the employer would have been too shy to tell him the company couldn't afford him, and he'd have lost the offer. He'd had to educate someone *inside* the company about the flexibility of salaries.

Remember, a company may not know what you know — that money can be fudged to fit the person.

No Experience

How do you determine your value if you think you're inexperienced?

The first such people who come to mind are recent college graduates. I recently read a survey of Harvard M.B.A. graduates whose biggest worry was that they didn't have any experience that would attract an employer.

Other "I don't have any experience" people are career changers, foreign immigrants, high-school students, even mainframe programmers switching to client-server networks.

Please be careful. Your tendency is to be so glad that someone is offering you a job that you accept with a beggar's nod and smile at whatever is offered. Ponder the following points.

If you followed Salary-Making Rules 1, 2, and 3, they're choosing *you*, not your price. They really want to hire *you!* They think you'll make or save them money.

Evidently you have the ability to do the work or the company wouldn't be making you an offer.

The company's hiring decision is based 95 percent on your personality, enthusiasm, and transferable skills. Only 5 percent has to do with your specialized knowledge. Since the company can't teach manners and common sense, the company *hires* it. Since it *can* teach its *subject,* it trains you. Therefore, 95 percent of you is experience worth bargaining about.

This is it! This is the only time you'll be at the starting line. Here's your chance to begin the virtuous cycle of Ms. Worth.

What do you have to lose?

So if you think you have no experience, remember the qualities that make you successful. To an offer of X dollars you'll say, "From my research, X dollars is around entry level for salary. Considering my enthusiasm and general success in the things I set out to do, I believe I'm worth about [a middle-of-range] Y dollars. What can you do in that area?"

When Do I Need to Talk to a Lawyer?

Dan Felix, a.k.a. "The Executive's Attorney," spoke to me about when it's a good idea to bring a lawyer into the negotiating mix.

The first strong indicator you need a lawyer was: anytime you're asked to actually sign anything – and, please, *before* you sign it, not afterwards.

If you're given something that sounds like *their* lawyer wrote it, let *your* lawyer read it. There's a strong probability you won't really know what it means! Sometimes, more important than telling you what's there, s/he can tell you what's *not* there; i.e. default provisions such as dispute resolution attorneys' fees, commission payments, etc. So, read it, of course, but have an attorney tell you what it really means.

What About the "nons"? Noncompete, Nondisclosure...

The man on the street might tell you, "Not to worry, they're not really enforceable." Wrong!

Non Compete, Non Disclosure, Non Solicitation, Non anything can all be enforceable and even if they aren't, it can cost big bucks to fight it later.

Go to www.SalaryNegotiations.com and I'll link you to more in-depth information from Dan about the "nons." For now, remember, if they try to slip it by you when you're signing your innocuous w-4 tax forms in personnel, wait. Think about whether what they're asking you to give up is worth it. And, since you can't understand that legalese, anyway, talk to a lawyer to know what, exactly, you're giving up.

Other Special Situations Call for Mr. Legalman

The following situations are examples of when to not only to have the agreement in writing, but to have it in writing in a way that's enforceable — hence, let a lawyer help you.

- When you've negotiated a valuable bonus, severance, stock option or other financial extra, especially if it's somehow different than what others in the company are already receiving. Memories can fade, even with the best of intentions. What was the exact performance or other event the bonus based on?

- When you're the first or only person in your position for your new employer. If you're the first marketing professional for an accounting firm, for example, getting the benefits of the expanded and detailed written contract process should help expectations on both sides, helping to ensure a successful tenure.

- When you're leaving a good position with a competitor, or having to relocate your residence, you'd be well advised to get written assurances of the security of your new position – and covering those many "what if's" and especially what if the new position doesn't work out.

- It is usually critical to get a written contract if you're bringing something to the table that you want to walk out with when you and your new employer [inevitably] part ways.

A written contract to cover this situation is important for several different groups. To name just a few: experienced sales people with their list of established clients and contacts as well as scientists and others who want to keep part of their inventions and other intellectual property. If you don't have a written contract, anything you bring to the table or develop while an employee, may well end up the property of your employer!

When in doubt, check it out.

By the way, there's two kinds of lawyers in this domain: the ones who work for the companies and the ones who work for the individual (plaintiff) – that's the kind you want. If you live in Illinois, you're in luck! Dan Felix can take good care of you -- go to my site, www.SalaryNegotiations.com, and you can find a link to his site there. If you're in any of the other 49 states, Dan's site still might be able to help you -- he's working on a list of attorneys you can rely on.

Negotiating a Severance Package: Background

Can you negotiate for money when you've been fired?

Four hundred fifteen thousand people were released from their jobs in the United States in 2004. As downsizings, RIFs, and mergers become more common, so also do severance packages for terminated employees. Employers offer them severance for two reasons.

First, when people are angry (as is often the case when they've been fired, especially if through no fault of their own), they want retribution; they often sue, or threaten to sue, their employers. Even though such suits are rarely successful, they are a nuisance. So employers will give some severance in consideration for a release.

Second, employers are people; people do have hearts. So if they can afford it, they would prefer to help the former employee find new work even if they have no strict obligation to do so.

A Word about Lawsuits.

Most states have employment "at-will" laws, which means that, as long as employers don't discriminate by race, creed, sex, age, certain disabilities, etc., or break any individual employment contract, they are free to hire and fire anyone they wish—and you're free to quit! While being fired is never pleasant when it happens to you, all in all the free-enterprise system runs better with this flexibility, and it makes it easier for the "system" to hire you somewhere else.

However, if you feel you actually have been discriminated against in your termination, you can consider suing, although it will decrease your employability somewhat even if you prevail. If you want to learn about your rights, you can call the National Employment Lawyers Association at (415) 227-4655.

Generally I counsel my clients not to sue, but to negotiate a severance instead. If you have strong discrimination grounds, or are simply in a discrimination category, you have better leverage to negotiate a severance than if you're a white, English-speaking male under forty.

Still, a lawsuit is seldom satisfying, even to the winner. In my opinion, you'd be better off to get a severance and go forward with your life. Get your "revenge" by negotiating a severance, taking the money, scoring a new job quickly, and laughing all the way to the bank.

Negotiating a Severance Package: Timing

Timing. Don't just accept the severance offer on the spot. Listen, then say, "I appreciate this, and will consider this carefully. When can we talk about this again in case I have any questions or requests?"

When you've been fired, separate your anger and resentment from your efforts to get a good severance package. Money won't change your feelings; it will just help your finances in transition. So make the best deal with that in mind, not as a way to retaliate against your employer. Take time to cool off.

Consult the laws of your state, check provisions of your union or other contract if you have one, and modify the following advice accordingly.

When you return after having thought about it (and having contacted a lawyer if doing so is relevant in your case – check my site for legal resources), negotiate the best package you can.

Negotiating Severance Timing II: Long before you need it.

By the way, the best time to negotiate severance is not when you're fired, but, rather, when you're hired. Kind of like the way a prenuptial agreement prevents nasty court battles if, alas, divorce occurs. So, also, getting your severance agreed upon at hiring time when the future looks rosy is much better than later when things took a turn for the worse. So, how does one tactfully bring up termination when getting hired? Set up the negotiation by using two softening positions:

- It's not *them* that you're worried about and

- there's nothing to lose.

It could go like this: "Mr. Employer, there's one small concern I have. I wonder if we could discuss it." [Of course!]

"Well, do you foresee a change in management, a merger, buy-out or change in ownership anywhere on the horizon?" [No!]

"Good. It's just that in times like these with takeovers, IPOs and competition from dot.coms, etc., sometimes a job can be going great and I could be performing well, and then, through no fault of my own, there's a chance I could be out on the street. So, you don't foresee this happening, is that right?" [No, no, that won't happen.] Notice softening position number one: you avoid implying you don't trust *them* by "blaming" potential involuntary termination on possible changes in the market or management.

"Well, then what I'm going to request shouldn't cost the company any money at all. Could we agree that in the unlikely event I'm involuntarily terminated (except for cause) that I could have ____ month's severance pay including medical benefits?" Notice softening position number two: if there's no changes in the foreseeable future, then severance won't cost them a cent!

Will you get it? Maybe. Maybe not. But it's worth asking! Six months is a good time frame. Ask for more if you feel it's justified.

There will likely be conditions – first of all that it applies only to getting fired, not quitting (called involuntary vs. voluntary termination). Also, you may need to agree to a severance package that activates only if termination occurs within a two- or three-year period, or upon termination pursuant to the sale/merger of the company, or change in management, but, obviously, it's always better for you if you can get it open-ended without conditions.

Like insurance, you hope you'll never have to invoke this clause, but, also like insurance, you'll be glad you have it if you need it.

Whether you're negotiating at the beginning, middle or end of your employment, here are the four elements of a severance package to keep in mind:

Negotiating Severance: Four Items

More Money

In most situations, employers aren't required to offer even two weeks' notice (severance), though they generally won't go below this unless you are terminated for cause.

Severance pay should be in addition to, not in lieu of, accrued vacation and personal time.

Generally speaking, the higher your rank, the more you can get. Four weeks for each year of service is extremely generous; be joyful at three; an employer's initial offer would probably be one or two. At executive levels, the weeks-for-years formula isn't as applicable. Middle managers should get three to four months' salary, and high-level executives should look for nine months to a year.

A way to get more money yet not have a package that looks bigger than anyone else's is to ask to delay your effective termination date. Even if you never come into the office again, your official termination date can be put off a few weeks, which will add a few more weeks' severance.

Bonuses and Commissions

Refer to the *Watch out!* paragraph in Chapter 7's "Sales Compensation" section. If you had the foresight to get "what commissions do I get paid if I'm no longer here" clear when you were hired, know exactly what's due now.

Whether or not you clarified this up front, you can still negotiate more now! If you have deals that are cooking and won't close without your tending, negotiate commissions you otherwise wouldn't get, in exchange for helping the company to close or keep the accounts despite your transition.

Bonuses are another matter. If there is a quarterly or annual trigger date for bonuses, and you're let go before that date, the company has no obligation to pay you the bonus. But you can ask! And if you can't get it all, maybe you can get some portion?

Letters of Recommendation

A nicely worded announcement praising your past contributions and expressing any company chagrin at having to let such a good employee go can help in your search. Don't worry too much about this, though; being fired doesn't carry the stigma it used to. Offer to give the company a letter for its editing, or ask to edit a letter given you by the company.

Now is the time to handle this, while the company is motivated to have a clean break; it would be harder to get a letter of reference later.

Job-Search Assistance: Outplacement

Most medium and large companies will pay for outplacement: job-search coaching and other ancillary job-search services. You may need to educate a smaller company about this benefit.

An important thing to negotiate here is your right to choose the provider. Don't worry too much about the costs; once you have interviewed a few firms, the one you pick will be able to negotiate with your personnel office to provide the best possible services within their budget.

Here are some criteria for choosing an outplacement provider. Choose a firm that will assign a personal counselor to work with you one on one. Ideally, its contract should obligate the firm to stay with you until you find a job, even if it takes a year or more. Ask to speak with the assigned counselor briefly to make sure the chemistry is right. Make sure your counselor has three or more years' experience doing this kind of work. If you want advice about this, call me. I can help you select a firm. 847-853-1046.

Here are some additional niceties. A full outplacement contract will provide office, phone, message service, printing and mailing of résumés, and correspondence. An outplacement firm will also have some research capabilities to help you find organizations that you'd like to work for.

If your parting ways is exceptionally amicable, a job-search desk and phone and secretarial extras can be provided by your (former) company, too. That could make outplacement counseling — the most important part — more affordable.

But be careful here; don't choose outplacement providers because you think they have more contacts than you do. Rather, evaluate and rely on their ability to help you make new contacts, i.e. to coach your self-presentation and networking well enough that appropriate hiring decision makers are eager to meet you. The power to make people interested in meeting you is much better than hoping that some of the firm's contacts will see you as a favor.

Negotiating by E-mail

Don't do it.

E-mail is 100% verbal; communication is 90% or more *non*verbal (inflection, pauses, facial expressions, etc.). You'll be entrusting thousands or even tens of thousands of dollars to a medium that employs only 10% of your communication abilities. Does "Yeah, right," mean "yes, indeed!" or "you can't be serious!"? Without non-verbals, you can't tell.

I coached Fred, who had a received an offer by email of $55,000 and benefits. He had replied by email to the president that he was not interested at that price, and to "take his hat out of the ring." Questioning him, I uncovered that "at that price" meant Fred had felt insulted by the president's "low" offer.

While it was true that the offer was a bit low, it was not true that the employer intended in any way to insult Fred. Upon deeper examination, we found misplaced anger: it was really Fred's frustration in the job search and upset at his previous employer's insults that got triggered and vented here. All because email can be interpreted as insulting when voice would be heard as acknowledging. Once these two "egos" got together face to face, it became clear how valuable each considered the other to be. Fred was able to negotiate a wonderful deal.

FWIW, IMHO (that's "e-mail speak" for "For What It's Worth, In My Humble Opinion"), it's tough enough to do this stuff real-space, real-time. Crippling the communications by subtracting all the non-verbals cannot do any good, and will probably do harm.

Voice to voice will do; face to face is better.

More Special Situations: see www.SalaryNegotiations.com

I've written about several other negotiations topics and situations on my website. Use BoughtTheBook as a password and you'll be able to get access to these articles, (and more).

- Are Bonuses Refundable?
- Be Willing to Walk Away
- Can My Employer Find Out How Much I am Making?
- Catching Up After Starting at a Low Salary

- Countering an Aggressive Employer
- Declining a Counter-Offer
- Deferred Compensation: Why wait?
- Does a Title Matter? Should I Negotiate it?
- Fixing Negotiation Mistakes
- Full time vs. Part time—Change in Pay?
- More About When to Get It In Writing
- More Work—Same Pay. Now What?
- Negotiating Health Benefits & Other Perks
- Negotiating Telecommuting
- Negotiations: Be Willing to Walk Away.
- Promotion or a Lateral Move?
- Salary Negotiations in a Slow Economy
- Squeezing Money Out of Hard Work and Good Luck
- Three Reasons to Decline a Counter-Offer
- Took a Low offer--Now what?
- Underpaid? Women & Salary Negotiations
- Using Internal Information About Salary
- Why Men Earn More & What To Do About It

Summary of Special-Situation Rules

- When discussing salary expectations outside job interviews, focus on a researched level of responsibility and concomitant pay.

- With recruiters and employment agents, even when you're discussing a specific job, you may go first, but if you can avoid it and still get the opportunity to interview, it can be to your advantage. Stress your researched expectations, not your present salary, and give a wide range.

- Use a researched range, too, when confronted with rigid salary structures. See whether you can get a new salary, based on your market value, within that structure.

- When you're getting "overqualified" feedback or hesitancy in bringing up salary, check on the status of the job offer and initiate salary discussions.

- When you think you haven't any experience, choose to start Ms. Worth's virtuous cycle.

- If you've been let go, don't go yet! Negotiate a severance.

- Better yet—negotiate severance in the hiring interview.

- BTW, IMHO, you should avoid negotiations by e-mail; HAND.

- Check with a Lawyer when it's complicated or risky.

- Go to www.SalaryNegotiations.com for more information

- [If you can get stock options or grants to own a piece of the rock, go for it! ...which brings us to the next chapter, "Stock Options Package."

Chapter 9
Evaluating And Negotiating A Stock Options Package

I asked Corey Rosen at the National Center for Employee Ownership [NCEO] to go into depth on the topic of negotiating stock options. This chapter is largely his work and you can dive even deeper in to the subject, if you wish, by getting a copy of his book.

The NCEO has numerous publications (check the website), and data about options allocation practices, and an extensive Web site at www.nceo.org. For more information, contact the NCEO at (510) 208-1300.

The Fundamentals

If you're like most people, you're excited to be getting stock options as part of your compensation, but you're also a bit confused by just how options work. You've had friends and colleagues who have received stock options, but you're not really sure how yours compare or how you can negotiate for a better options package. This chapter is intended to help you make sense of what you are being offered and give you ideas on what things might or might not be negotiable.

There is simply too much variation between companies and employees within companies to provide a "hard-and-fast" negotiation strategy for stock options. Instead, the goal here is to help you understand how options packages vary so that you will be ready to have an intelligent discussion, understanding both your and your employer's concerns. This chapter will first provide an overview of stock options, their tax treatment, and why they can be valuable. It will then discuss why and how companies grant stock options, and finally, review some key considerations in evaluating and negotiating your options package.

Part 1: Stock Options 101: What Is a Stock Option?

A stock option gives you the right to purchase a certain number of shares of stock in your company for a fixed price. It is a contract between you and the company, subject to certain terms and conditions. The options expire on a certain date, meaning that you only have a certain period of time in which to purchase the shares (also known as "exercising" the options). This is usually ten years. Options are also subject to vesting, a process through which you gradually earn a right to purchase the shares, For instance, you might be 20% vested after one year, 40% after two, 60% after three, 80% after four, and 100% after five years. This means that after two years, you would have the right to exercise 40% of the options.

The price at which you can purchase the shares is usually the fair market price at the time of the grant. With a stock option, you decide when to purchase the shares and when to sell. You cannot lose with an option. If the share price never goes over the grant price, you can simply choose not to purchase the shares. The simplest way to purchase the shares is with cash. Most companies also have "cashless" exercise mechanisms that allow you to receive the shares without actually spending cash. The most popular of these are broker-assisted purchases and sales, company loans, and stock swaps.

In a simple example, you might receive stock options that give you the right to purchase 1,000 shares at $10 per share for the next ten years and that vest 25% every year for four years. Seven years later, the share price is at $30, so you decide to purchase the shares. The $20 spread on each share is your gain.

Taxes and the Two Different Types of Options

The gain that you recognize with a stock option is subject to tax. There are two different types of stock options, each with a different tax treatment.

Nonqualified Stock Options (NSOs)

Nonqualified stock options (NSOs) do not qualify for any special tax treatment from the IRS. There are no legal limits of how many options people can get, nor are there any requirements for how they should be given out. Companies have complete discretion. Different employees, even doing the same job, can get different option packages.

When employees exercise a nonqualified option, they pay ordinary income tax on the spread between the grant price and the price on the date of exercise. That spread is treated like part of your compensation, and you pay the same taxes as if it were part of your regular paycheck. Your company would get a tax deduction for the same amount. *This is true whether you actually sell the shares or not.*

If you hold onto the shares after exercise, any additional gain between the price at the time of exercise and the price at the time of sale is treated as a capital gain. There are two capital gains tax rates. Short-term capital gains rates are the same as ordinary income tax rates, but long-term capital gains rates are lower than ordinary income tax rates. To receive long-term capital gains treatment, you have to hold onto the stock for at least one year after exercise before sale.

For example, an individual making $110,000 per year exercises 1,000 nonqualified options at $10 per share for stock worth $25. The individual must report a gain subject to ordinary income tax of $15 x 1,000 ($15,000) and pay 31% tax on that amount. If the shares are then held for another two years and go up another $5 per share, this additional gain of $5,000 would be subject to long-term capital gains.

Incentive Stock Options (ISOs)

Incentive stock options are more complicated, but offer the possibility of better tax treatment for employees. When an employee exercises an ISO they do not pay any tax. When they later sell the shares, they will pay capital gains taxes on the entire spread. Companies do not take a tax deduction for ISOs.

In order to qualify for this better tax treatment, ISOs must comply with certain regulations. Most importantly, the employee must hold the shares for at least one year after the date of exercise and two years after the date of grant. The company must also comply with specific rules in terms of how ISOs are granted.

For example, an individual making $110,000 per year exercises 1,000 incentive stock options at $10 per share for stock worth $25. If the shares are held for at least 12 months after exercise, and go up another $5 per share, for a total gain of $20,000, the total amount ($25 - $10) would be subject to capital gains taxes of 20%, or $4,000.

There is another catch. The exercise of an ISO may also subject optionees to something called the alternative minimum tax (AMT). The AMT was enacted to prevent higher-income taxpayers from paying too little tax because they are able to take a variety of tax deductions or exclusions. The AMT requires that taxpayers who may be subject to it calculate their taxes in two ways. First, they figure out how much tax they would using the normal tax rules. Then, they add back in to their taxable income certain deductions and exclusions they took when figuring their regular tax and, using this now higher number, calculate the AMT. If the AMT is higher, the taxpayer pays that tax instead.

The spread between the grant price and the price at the time of exercise is one of the "preference items" that must be added back into the AMT calculation. In many situations when employees pay the AMT because of the exercise of ISOs, they will get most of it back in the future. The amount by which the AMT exceeds your regular tax payment becomes a "minimum tax credit" (MTC) that can be applied in future years when normal taxes exceed the AMT amount.

This explanation is the simplified version of a potentially complex matter. Anyone potentially subject to the AMT should use a tax advisor to make sure everything is done appropriately. If you receive ISOs take care to consider if you are subject to these rules.

With an ISO, it is also important to emphasize that you do not *have* to meet the holding periods. You only have to meet the holding periods to receive the favorable tax treatment. If you fail to meet the holding period requirements, then the option is just treated like an NSO. This is known as a "disqualifying disposition. You pay ordinary income tax on the spread between the grant price and the price at exercise and then capital gains on the rest. Since you are disqualifying, you are not holding on to the stock for one year, so you also pay short-term capital gains rates.

What Is It Really Worth?

The ultimate financial benefit of a stock option to you is the difference between the price at which you purchase the stock and the price at which you eventually sell the stock, minus the appropriate taxes. Maximizing this value, however, is not an easy decision. The decisions about when to exercise and when to sell depend on your beliefs about the stock price, tax consequences, and your tolerance for risk. Most economists would argue that to maximize the value of an option, you shouldn't exercise your options early, but hold on until nearly the end of the exercise term, exercising at a point prior to that when you feel the stock is relatively high.

That's easy for them to say. If you are sitting on an unexercised option that has gained considerable value, it's tempting to consolidate your gains. It's even more tempting if the market has been volatile for your company's shares or you need the money for something important. The economists are usually right, however. Assume you have an option to buy at $10 and the stock is at $25 six years later. If you exercise at $25, you either hold onto the shares and pay no taxes until sale (if it an ISO) or pay taxes now (if it is an NSO). In either event, you have paid $10 per share, and, if you pay taxes, probably another $3 or $4 per share as well. So you have between $10 per share and $14 per share that's been spent. That money isn't available to invest in other things. By contrast, if you wait to exercise, it is. It's a strong argument, but one you need to evaluate in terms of the tax consequences, other investment opportunities, financial goals, and assessment of the risk of waiting.

Part 2: The Company's Perspective

Understanding the company's perspective should give you a better basis for understanding why your company is granting you stock options and the constraints on the company in offering this form of reward. Armed with this knowledge, you are in a better position to see why your option package is what it is and, if you are attempting to negotiate a better package, how you might improve it.

Why Pay in Options at All When There's Always Cold, Hard Cash?

Why would companies go to all this hassle to provide options to employees? First, some companies don't have the cash. This applies mostly to small start-ups that need to conserve every dollar to keep operating. They may, in effect, make a deal with employees to accept a right to a share of the future growth of the company instead of a more competitive salary. Second, companies may have enough cash on hand, but prefer to use it to fund growth. Most of these companies are already paying a competitive wage, but want to provide employees with something extra.

A third incentive for paying in options is that a quirk in accounting rules provides that companies do not have to show any current expense on their income statement when they issue employees options, although there are a few exceptions.

Fourth, companies pay in options because employees demand them. Over the last quarter century, real wages have increased hardly at all, while returns to shareholders have gone up at a rate much faster than any time in history. Employees have figured out that the road to wealth lies through ownership. Finally, companies see options as a way to tie employees to the company, to give them an interest in helping the company perform better.

How Companies Grant Stock Options

Companies have a great deal of flexibility in how they grant stock options. There are few rules and regulations about who gets options, how many, and how often.

Some companies grant to everyone, others grant to employees at certain levels, others grant to only managers or executives. It is entirely up to the company. As for as the timing of grants, most companies, especially in the high-tech sector, grant options to employees when they are hired. Many companies supplement these new hire grants with ongoing grants. Another common granting practice is to grant options to employees at one time for individual performance or as part of a larger company-wide grant.

In terms of how many options employees receive, it is also entirely up to the company. Most often, the number of options depends on your position in the company. Like salary, in general, the higher up your position, the more options you will receive.

For new hire grants, the amount given to new employees is usually driven by competitive considerations: how much do we need to give to get someone to do this job considering what other companies are doing? Often these grants are substantial, and there may be significant variation even within a company. You may be able to negotiate the option package you receive at the time of hire, especially if you have skills and experience that are in serious demand.

Ongoing grants are often based on getting promoted or performance reviews. Here there may be room to negotiate as part of a performance contract ("if I can do this, I will get this number of options"). Other companies may grant options based on the achievement of corporate or group targets, in which case there is usually a set formula for who will get what. Finally, many plans grant options solely at the discretion of a group leader, management, or the company's board of directors. Here too there may be room for negotiation if you feel you have leverage with the company.

For most one-time, company wide grants, all employees get the same number of stock options. This approach is most common in very large companies. Of course, these approaches are not mutually exclusive, and plans may often include elements of more than one approach.

Part 3: Evaluating and Negotiating Your Option Agreement

The most important factor that will determine the value of your options is the performance of the company's stock price, something that is not negotiable. There are certain terms and conditions of the option agreement, however, you may be able to negotiate. Here are some of the more important terms.

How Many Options Should You Get and What Does That Mean?

This is a very important and difficult question. A smaller number of options in a company with very good growth prospects may be just as or more valuable than a large number of options in a company growing more slowly. The risk that the options will be worth anything at all varies too. Here, however, are some of the factors you need to consider in evaluating what the number of options you are offered means. There is data available from the NCEO and other organizations about how options are allocated in various kinds of companies. You can use this as a very rough guide to see how your peers fare, but these data should be viewed with considerable caution.

Are you better off working for a company that gives you 100, 1,000, or 10,000 options? The answer is you cannot say from just this information. If you get 10,000 options at $1, 1,000 options at $10, or 100 options at $100, you have the same current economic value. Consider this example. Assume that company A gives you 10,000 options at $1, Company B 1,000 options at $10, and Company C 100 options at $100. Assume further than each company's stock price grows 10% over the next seven years. Factoring in the compound rate of growth on this, your stock would just about double in that time. To make it simple, we'll assume it does. Here is what you would have:

Company A: 10,000 options at $1.

Option price = $1

Purchase price = $2

Net gain = 10,000 x $1 ($2 per share - $1 per share) = $10,000

Company B: 1,000 options at $10

Option price = $10

Purchase price = $20

Net gain = $1,000 x $10 ($20 per share - $10 per share) = $10,000

Company C: 100 options at $100

Option price = $100

Purchase price = $200

Net gain = 100 x $100 ($200 per share - $100 per share) = $10,000

In other words, the number of options is not the key calculation. It is the number of options times the price at which the options are granted that fixes the "face" value of the option. But this calculation leaves much to be desired. It's really only a starting point. Several other factors affect just how to assess the value of the number of options you have.

Company Risk

How likely is it that the company will even be around in a few years? And if it is, what is the chance its share price will go up, and if so, by how much? There is no easy way to answer these questions. In general, the riskier the company, the greater the potential gain. With a lot of options in a risky company, you could strike it rich – or end up with zero. You could end up somewhere in the middle too. In a more stable company with a steadily growing stock price, you are much more likely to end up somewhere in the middle.

Volatility

Probably nothing surprises option holders more than to learn that options are generally worth *more* in companies with volatile stock. With a volatile stock, the price experiences lots of ups and downs, as opposed to a stock that is not volatile, which grows or declines in a much more stable, incremental fashion. An option gives you the chance to exercise at the high points and lets you ignore the low ones. There is also, however, the risk that some volatile companies may go out of business altogether.

Will You Get More Options in the Future?

The options you get when you join the company hopefully are not the last you will get. Structuring an agreement so that you can get additional options over time is a critical negotiating issue. In fact, you may not want to get all your options up front. If you get all or most of your options early on, you have entered a lottery. If the price was historically very high, your options may turn out to be not worth much. You would be better off in this scenario if you got options periodically, some at $100, some at the dip next year when the stock went to $60, and so on. You average out your risk this way.

Type of Option

In general, it's better for you to have ISOs than NSOs. You don't have to pay taxes right away, so you may be able to hold on to at least some of the shares. On the other hand, if the AMT is going to effect you, or you are already in a very low tax bracket, this advantage may be negligible. It's worth asking for ISOs in most cases, especially in start-up companies where taxes for the company are not going to be an issue for the foreseeable future. Most companies, however, are not likely to want to bargain on this issue.

The Exercise Period

The longer the term of your option (the number of years you have to exercise it), the more valuable it is. If you can continue to buy stock at $10 for ten years, that is obviously worth a lot more than a right to buy for only five. While this is a critical factor, it may be a tough one to negotiate. Companies rarely give different people different terms.

Vesting

Employees gradually receive a right to exercise their stock options through a process known as vesting. Vesting schedules are usually fixed for everyone. Most companies vest options over a period of three to five years. Vesting does not always proceed evenly across the years. Some companies provide equal vesting, 25% per year, for instance. Others may vest a large share each year. Some companies vest a little every quarter or even every month, usually so that people will not exercise their options all at the same time each year. More frequent vesting events also can provide employees better opportunities, especially in volatile companies where employees may want to exercise their options quickly to take advantage of market fluctuations. Like the length of the option term, however, companies will rarely negotiate a different vesting schedule.

Transfer Rights

Stock options can only be transferred to other parties if the plan specifically allows it. Companies are generally not eager to offer transfer rights broadly to employees, however, even to their family members. Usually, this right is granted, if at all, only to key people.

Selling Your Shares in a Closely Held Company

If your company is publicly traded, shares you purchased through stock options can be sold on a stock exchange. What if your company is not publicly traded? How do you sell your shares? There are three common provisions for this in closely held companies. In many cases, options can be exercised at any time they are vested, but the shares can only be sold if the company goes public or is sold. A second approach is to provide an internal market for the shares, either by having the company buy them or other individuals, often employees, buy them. Finally, the company may agree to buy any shares only at the price they were granted unless the company is sold or goes public.

From the company standpoint, the first approach is preferable because it has the least cost. From your standpoint, the second makes the most sense, with the third being in the middle. But if the shares are purchased internally, you need to understand and be comfortable with how a value is set for the shares.

Change of Control and IPOs

What happens to your stock options when the company is sold (a "change of control" transaction) or goes public (an "initial public offering").

When a company is sold, there is no standard answer, but some important considerations. The first is whether your unvested options will vest on change of control. Most of the time, unvested options vest fully on a change of control. However, some plans leave the matter up to the discretion of the board of directors, while others cancel any unvested shares.

The second consideration is when and to whom will you be able to sell the shares that from exercised options. In most cases, they will be purchased by the acquiring company as part of the transaction. Because there is no legal requirement that plans provide this, however, a plan could provide that the shares will be purchased at a later date or that employees will get shares in the acquisition company in their place. If these are publicly traded shares, this is not a problem, but if they are shares of a closely held company, you may not be able to sell them

The final consideration here is whether your options will be exchanged for options in the new company, a common approach. Existing options generally would carry forward their vesting and exercise terms, but not necessarily. Generally, the options exchange is supposed to be for equal value, although this can be a complex issue.

If a company does a public offering, the issues are usually more straightforward. Options typically simply continue their vesting and exercise terms, but now the shares are more liquid. However, securities rules prohibit the sale of shares obtained through options exercises for certain employees (generally, top executives). In some cases, the company and/or its investors and investment bankers (those who arrange the transaction to go public) may establish rules that prevent the sale of shares from options for defined periods of times.

As with other aspects of options, these issues may or may not be negotiable, but, in general, issues concerning change of control may be more negotiable than other issues. In any event, it is important at least to have a clear understanding of what will happen in these cases and have specific language in your option grant covering them. Otherwise, you are leaving these events purely to the discretion of whoever controls the company at the time these events occur.

Conclusion

There is a great deal to consider in understanding and, if possible, negotiating an options package. It may seem daunting to go through all this, and tempting just to trust the plan to be set up properly and fairly. There is a good chance it will be, of course. But some plans may simply overlook certain important issues that, if brought to the attention of management, they will agree need to resolve. In other cases, terms may not be what you would like, but they were carefully thought about and may be difficult to change, but you can't know until you ask.

If your options package is substantial, and you are at all uncertain about it, it may be advisable to seek professional advice, usually an attorney or accountant familiar with these plans. The cost may be well worth the results.

Corey Rosen's forthcoming book on evaluating and negotiating a stock options package was not yet in print (or even titled) as of the December, 2000 printing of this book. Check the website mentioned at the beginning of this chapter for more information on his book.

Chapter 10
Raises and Salary Reviews

Why Would Your Boss Give You a Raise?

If you want a higher salary for your present job, it behooves you to answer this question: Why would anybody want to give somebody a raise?

By "raise," I don't mean a cost-of-living adjustment (COLA) to keep pace with inflation. If you've read "Negotiating Bennies and Perks" in Chapter 7, you realize that's no raise. When consumer prices are climbing, most workers' raises have, in reality, just helped them keep pace with inflation. Let's look back at relatively high inflation years.

The first version this book was published about 1988, and inflation in the United States was 4.4 percent, and for the four years after was 4.6, 6.1, 3.1, and 2.9 percent, respectively. [You can do the same type of math for 2000 – 2006 inflation stats.] That totals 21.1 percent by simple addition. But it's really more than that because inflation, like interest on savings accounts, compounds. So for 1988-93, inflation actually cut purchasing power almost 23 percent!

For example, if you earned $30,000 in 1988 and $36,875 in 1993, you didn't receive a raise at all. You would need in 1993 to have earned almost one and a quarter times your 1988 salary just to maintain the same buying power.

But wait. It's even worse than that!

In 1988 your income was taxed in the thirty-grand bracket. Now you're paying taxes on nearly thirty-seven grand so probably are in a higher tax bracket. That means we're talking about a 23-to-40-percent increase in pay needed over five years *just to buy the same house, clothes, and food as before.* The numbers for low inflation years, like 1998-2000 are still a hefty amount, eh?

With inflation that high, why would anybody want to give somebody a raise, too?

The answer is that employers don't *give* raises, employees *earn* them.

Remember the *Make me a buck* principle? Here's a corollary: The longer you are in a particular job, the better you perform it (one hopes). The better you perform it, the more goods and services you produce in that same forty-hour week, therefore the more value you're producing for your employer. *So, since you're making the employer more bucks, a raise is just your fair share of those bigger profits.*

If you think you deserve a raise just for reporting to work each of last year's 251 workdays, you're mistaken. People act as if they're *entitled* to a raise every year but, from your employer's perspective, continued increases in salary without increases in value merely make you a prime target for the next layoffs. During the last recession, that happened to many managers who were being overpaid for the amount of work they did. They were either let go or encouraged to retire.

Earning It

At first glance, continually boosting your output might look like an overwhelming task. You may wonder just how much more productive you'd have to be to earn a raise. Say you're in the same job for ten years and need to accomplish more each year.

You might reach a point where you think, "I can't do any more than I'm already doing!"

But that's not so. If you set your sights correctly, you can contribute more every single year than you did the year before. I'm not talking about working harder, I'm talking about working *smarter*. If you put your brain to it, you can actually work less time and accomplish more. And there are no upper limits, especially in the new millennium when there are countless ways that electronics can "chip away" at many of the time-consuming tasks of yesteryear. And there's never a limit to the satisfaction and commitment you can create in co-workers, management, customers, and vendors.

Although you do need to be more valuable, you don't need to double your output to net a 5-percent raise. A solid record of good work is all that's required. If your mind is active and engaged in your job, productivity increases will happen automatically. All you need to do is notice them.

Since the focus of this book is salary and raise negotiating, this chapter concentrates on *negotiating* raises you've earned rather than *earning* raises to negotiate. The latter—performing on the job in such a way that you deserve a raise—is a book in itself. Two books, in fact, and a tape set:

- Richard Germann: Working and Liking It

- Steve Kravette: Get a Raise in 60 Days

- Jack Chapman (me!): How to Beat the System and Get a Raise! (Tape Set & Workshop Manual)

The two books are old, but the best I've seen. Amazon.com can locate copies for you. You'll find more info in "Resources" section in the back of this book.

Richard Germann's book takes you through a program to create an ideal job out of your present one. It covers analyzing your best talents, establishing a contact-and-information network within your company, defining your ideal situation, gaining recognition for your worth, and launching a step-by-step campaign using research, communication, and persuasion.

Steve Kravette's book teaches you the attitude and performance you need to get a raise at any time you want one, without working overtime or changing company policies.

Each is a powerful book that I recommend for strategies on earning a promotion or raise.

**Figure 10-1. Employers don't give raises.
Employees earn them.**

My tape set adds a very practical and motivational element to the ideas presented in Mr. Kravette's book. The set includes a workbook and taped exercises to turn his ideas into an easily implemented, almost foolproof way to get a raise. The tapes also augment some of the raise-negotiating techniques that follow.

Communication Is the Key

Now we'll learn how to *negotiate*. Let's assume you've kept your shoulder to the wheel all year long. You have thrown every morsel of energy, creativity, and positive mental attitude humanly possible into your job. You have made your company a bundle.

How do you negotiate a raise? Communication. Here are three communication steps:

1) Document your results;

2) Get your boss to acknowledge them;

3) Negotiate a raise the same way you'd negotiate a salary.

According to the saying "The wheel that squeaks the loudest is the one that gets the grease," a complainer may get more notice than you do. Don't assume that your boss knows what a good job you've done to keep things running so smoothly. Bosses who allow efficient workers the freedom to do a good job are *less* likely to be aware of workers' accomplishments! Such bosses are so trusting of your work that they naturally pay attention to their problems instead of your performance. They aren't motivated to delve into your accomplishments. Therefore, you'll have to delve for them.

The best way to do that is to keep a job journal. If your review is due soon, start your journal by reviewing the period since your last raise and writing down the most significant things you've done. If your review is a long time off, begin your journal today and it will be your magic carpet to Raiseland later. Start by purchasing a spiral notebook big enough to hold large entries and small enough to tuck into a very accessible place.

I'm indebted to Carl Armbruster, a Massachusetts career counselor, for the following description of a job journal, a splendid tool for negotiating raises.

A journal can assist your career in a number of ways, but none of them is magical. You have to work at career advancement, and a journal gives you excellent material to accomplish the task.

What do you write in your career log? There are four kinds of observations. The first kind is about your achievements. As you work you are solving certain problems, learning new techniques, creating new approaches.   Record these small triumphs in your journal, with enough factual information to describe exactly what happened and what the results were.

Quantifiable data such as approximate percentages, rounded dollar figures, or units of time are especially desirable. Achievements don't have to be earth-shaking (you weren't hired to be a miracle worker), but they should be tangible evidence of your effectiveness on the job.

The second set of observations comes from time spent studying your superiors, colleagues, subordinates, or customers. Start a policy of observing people in order to find out what their strongest talents are. Don't look for weaknesses or chinks in their armor, because negative appraisals don't lead anywhere.   They just sour you on the people.

But a positive observation of what their skills are can help you respect them and thus lay a firm foundation for building good human relations. Also, you will know more precisely how to approach them effectively to get their support for your projects, promotions, or raises. Your notebook forces you to be aware of them.

The third set of observations includes your ideas for progress. How often have you had the experience of getting a brilliant insight into how to do your job better or to create something more efficient and then two weeks later find that you're unable to recall the idea that had excited you so much? Since they may be lost due to the frailty of human memory, insights of genius should be recorded.

The fourth kind of observation includes news items, information, or sources of information about your chosen career field, such as newspaper and magazine articles. You want to be professional and keep up with what's going on. Your reading in your field should be documented for future use.

Using a Job Journal

For documenting your results, use your journal in step one of negotiating a raise.

A few weeks before your review, look through (or if you don't have a journal, think through) the first kind of observations: your achievements since your last raise. Especially note the differences between what you're doing now and what you did when you started at your current salary. Measure your achievements with respect to dollars, people, productivity, exposure, or anything else countable or measurable.

Analyzing your work with respect to measurable results gives you a concrete success agenda to share with your raise giver and shows you how you've actually been spending the time that, in effect, the employer buys from you.

In analyzing your results, take the raise-givers' viewpoint. What matters to them? What puts more money in their paychecks or bonuses? What will they be able to parlay into their own raises or promotions? What do they care deeply about?

For example, you were tired of being bugged repeatedly about the same old tripe by every new employee. So you organized a training program for the new people who come into your department. As a result these people now know what they're doing. But what counts to your boss? The boss is interested that your training program cuts 50 percent off the time he previously wasted on getting recruits up to speed. *And* that you were able to give 50 percent more of your own time to other money-making work because you didn't have to answer ridiculous questions every ten minutes.

This is where the second set of observations comes into play. Read through (or think about) the things that matter to your boss. These aren't always related to money. Bosses can also care about neatness, safety, morale, confidentiality, corporate visibility, efficiency, creativity, good press, or even fancy titles and time for golf. Knowing what your boss values will help you measure your results in language he or she will understand and appreciate. If you don't know what your boss considers important, ask!

Then take time to fill out pages similar to the Review Preparation Worksheet in figure 10-2. Use a separate page for each achievement you've had since your last salary increase. Later, come up with goals for yourself for the next year. You can use the ideas section from your journal. As an example, say your idea is to start up a chocolate-ice-cream break at 10:00 each morning. If you have a chocoholic boss, you're fine. Otherwise, project how much more work will get done, in the short or long term, so the discussion will have some merit.

Observations from the fourth section of your journal, news in your field, may also generate goals.

The Prereview Memo

When you've assembled that material, put together a prereview memo. Communication-step 2, you'll recall, is to get your boss to acknowledge your achievements. That can come only out of a personal meeting; just sending the memo will do precious little. But do *send* the memo. Hard-copy *not* e-mail. Make it one page. You can have a multipage document for backup purposes, but a one-page version has a simple, unique advantage over a longer one: Your boss will actually read it!

Achievement:

_____

_____

_____

Results (specifying money made or saved, time saved, percent improvement, etc.):

_____

_____

_____

Value these results have to my boss (and why my boss
would care about them):

_____

_____

_____

New problems or goals arising from this situation:

_____

_____

_____

Figure 10-2. Review Preparation Worksheet

Start the memo by thanking your boss for the opportunity to work and contribute to the organization over the past X months or year. Since your review is coming up (you continue), you've prepared a summary of the highlights during the period, which you expect to lead to a conversation about the next X months' or year's goals. Then, in bulleted form, list your top five areas of achievement. Make them brief, positive, and results oriented.

Each area will correspond to one of three types: **"Good show," "Nice going," or "Could've been worse."**

"Good show" is work you've done that directly affected the quality of products or services, or the quantity of profit or services. For example: Solidified communications with the independent distributors in Midwest region through personal visits and follow-up telephone work. Results: Sales increased 37 percent over last year and distributor turnover went down 20 percent."

In contrast to the measurable increase of "Good show," **"Nice going"** focuses on your ability to handle the routine stuff. Don't take the ordinary responsibilities of your job for granted. Remind your boss of the benefits that come from your simply doing your job right. For example, "Oversaw word-processing unit, hiring and training sixteen operators over the past year and maintaining the supplies and equipment. Results: You [the boss] have had, I believe, a completely worry-free year with regard to word processing, and no complaints of any substance from the staff."

The last category, **"Could've been worse,"** notes what at first you might regard as failures. For example: "Lost three major clients," "Produced 30-percent-fewer parts," "Turnover doubled," "Profits declined," or "We're really in debt now!" However, if you've been working hard, there is probably a case for "Things could've been worse." Mention the circumstances under which you were working (careful: no blaming, just facts), and turn plights into accomplishments. For example: "Retained 50 percent of my staff during the past year despite salary reductions and layoffs. I have a committed group who will dedicate themselves to the company's effort to survive this recession and keep your division strong and ready for the next steps."

End the memo with a comment about how you look forward to a productive discussion. *Do not mention raises in the memo.*

Send the memo seven to ten days before your review.

To whom do you send it? The way this particular memo is constructed, it goes only to your reviewer. If you are far enough ahead of schedule (a month or so), you can take some of the same journal material and send it as a report to several managers. The purpose, of course, is to let people know about your good work, but the best way to do that is to make it a request for feedback. Prepare the one-page memo or summary and include backup pages with some details on how you achieved your results and an honest presentation of questions that occurred to you while you prepared the material.

Nothing in life is so cut and dried that there aren't a few other options, a few worries about consequences, or a set of other considerations in our decision making. Getting other people's input on our decisions, albeit hindsight, is a way to be even more productive in the future. So send it out and invite discussion. Follow it up on your own in a week. Remember, if you do your work so well that nobody notices, nobody *will* notice!

Here's a case history of successfully sending a prereview memo to several managers.

Jack was in charge of preventive maintenance at a medium-size plant that manufactured tin cans. He did a great job. But until he documented his results, he didn't know how great.

By looking up the production records for the years before he was hired, Jack discovered how much money had been spent on repairs and how much had been lost due to production-line downtime.

He listed the new procedures he'd put into place: methods for machine maintenance, critical wear-testing of parts, and the gathering of input from production-line employees. He documented several of the improvements and tagged each with an estimated dollar savings. They totaled an astounding $200,000!

Jack decided that, since he'd been unaware of the extent of his own contribution, his bosses must be doubly unaware. And since preventive maintenance means doing things so nothing breaks, Jack was in exactly the kind of success-is-having-nobody-notice-anything position that further guarantees that higher-ups are oblivious to one's work.

During his first year, he did have to cope with breakdowns, malfunctions, and downtime, but these were a carry-over from his predecessor's shoddy work. His program's effectiveness wouldn't really show up until the next year!

His memo listed "Good show" for improvements in the equipment, the efficiency of operations, and the retrofitting of a machine that would have cost $80,000 to replace.

"Nice going" included his record of the past six months, such as recording and analyzing data about when and how things broke, and initiating the this-machine-is-sounding-strange reports from the line that would pay off by catching things before they broke.

He had a "Could've been worse" on a breakdown that stopped production for eight hours. He pointed out that he was able to cut the normal sixteen-hour repair time in half.

Jack sent the report to several people in a sincere effort to gather even more ideas and suggestions. He got them. One was a terrific idea about rewards for employees who find potential trouble spots, which served as fodder for the next year's review.

Jack and I discussed the $200,000 in savings. We noted that it was pure profit, the equivalent of earnings generated by $2 million to $4 million in sales.

In Jack's case, management actually came to him and gave him an increase plus bonuses equal to a 50-percent raise. Of course, the boss doesn't always step forward like that, so let's get back to you.

At the Negotiating Table

For your review, make sure you have undisturbed time to go over your memo with the boss. Bring your own copy. Begin the discussion by going over your contributions. Either you'll hear the boss acknowledge your effectiveness or you'll have to ask for it. One way or another, get the boss to agree that you are effective! Otherwise you'll have earned a raise in deeds, but not in the place that counts: the boss's mind.

Then get the boss in line with your goals, to see if the ideas you've hatched fit into his or her plans. Such a discussion will happen pretty naturally, but at the end request some clarity about whether the boss *wants* you to do these things. Be direct. Ask, "Are these goals important to you, and should I work on the them?" Or: "How would you rank these in order of importance? Should I start on number one first?"

At this point, as in salary negotiating, you've coaxed your employer as close to the judgit stage as possible. Therefore, as in salary negotiating, *let the boss name the figure first.*

You may, if you wish, first educate the boss on the difference between a raise and a COLA. You still won't be naming a figure first, but you'll be indirectly stating that you expect your increase to do more than just keep pace with inflation. You could say, "The cost-of-living adjustment this year is X percent; I'd like to discuss what my raise will be."

As in salary negotiating you absolutely *must* know the market value for comparable positions. Your ability to strike a bargain at the top of the range depends on it. In a salary negotiation, the question of disclosing your present or past salary is important. In a raise negotiation, that point is moot; obviously, your boss already knows your present salary. Therefore, the most important thing is knowing your market value. You acquire that knowledge by researching two types of sources: external and internal.

Use the other resources described in Chapter 5 to come up with a market value externally. By using a hard copy of your Pay-Comparison Analysis Report or other printed sources, or both, you can gain leverage with your boss in this discussion.

Internally, make sure you nose around and find out whatever you can about compensation policies and practices and the current profitability and operating budget of your division, company, or organization. That will be useful for comparing your salary with others outside the company.

It's tempting to use your market knowledge and documentation of your value to come up with a figure and go first. *Don't*. You may think that declaring a value 20 percent above your present compensation will prompt the company to budge from its 2-percent plans, and it probably would. But if the company intended to *double* your salary, do you think it'd go that high knowing you'd be tickled with less? Let your boss sweat. If you've made the best case for your value, quote Elwood P. Dowd and say, "What did you have in mind?"

When you hear 2 percent, repeat it, look glum for thirty seconds, and respond by reporting your research. "I've spent some time looking into the current market value of this type of position," you say, "and my research indicates a range from X dollars to Y dollars. I'm not sure if you were aware of that. Considering my contributions that we've just discussed, I think a fair salary would be in the Y-dollar vicinity." If the boss seems skeptical, you could present documentation of your research in a manila folder for him/her to look at then, or later. (See the section on research and pay-comparison analyses in Chapter 5.)

Remember, too, that fringe bennies and perks can easily compensate if your employer can't move the base. An extra week of vacation, for example, is a 2-percent raise. Look over the list of bennies and perks in Figure 7-1. Determine which ones you could ask for, then ask.

From that point, you're on your own. Come up with a salary that is fair and will keep you committed and productive.

Creating Raises and Promotions

Don't just wait for reviews and anniversaries to ask for a raise, either. An ideal time to get an increase is when changes occur at work. When you do a tremendous job on a revenue-producing project, when you take on more work because someone quits and the position isn't filled, any time your value to the organization increases, take the opportunity to send a brief memo to your boss and discuss compensation. You may negotiate a one-time bonus, a raise, or, when your job changes significantly, something besides a raise (which is usually based on your last salary): a new *salary* appropriate to your new *job*.

Sometimes a new job just creeps up on you. When you document your accomplishments, notice how your job has evolved. Have you begun making decisions only the boss made before? Did the part-time help you hired to handle the rush turn into a full-time staff of one-and-a-half people you now train and supervise? Are you now selling to customers you previously only serviced?

Do some subtraction. This year's responsibilities minus last year's responsibilities may yield a big remainder. It's called a new job. Instead of a raise, it deserves a whole new salary based on its actual value to the company.

Naturally, most employers will continue seeing you as your old self. So you're going to have to educate someone about your new position. Otherwise, your boss is likely to think that the jump from $30,000 to $45,000 a year is a 50-percent raise, when actually it's a new salary appropriate to your new job.

The *clearest* way to break the box your employer thinks you're in is to invent a new job title. For example, it'd be easier to get the salary of an "accounting-services coordinator" than the raise of an "accounting clerk." Don't, however, call it a promotion. Promotions sometimes have to be reviewed and approved. Yours has already occurred, and it's just as real as a formal promotion, so don't buy the line "We'll see if we can promote you."

You say, "I don't care about a title as much as simply being paid market value for the work I contribute here."

Now you've *negotiated* a raise, or even a promotion; you're feeling proud of yourself. I can tell you from experience with many clients that that will definitely start you on the virtuous cycle of Ms. Worth. You'll win, your employer will win, and your future will be even brighter.

Chapter 11
You Go First **Perspective**

When *You Go First* Is Safe

I saved these *You go first* comments for the end because, since it is easier to go first than it is to follow Salary Rule 1, *Postpone salary discussions until you have been offered the job,* I didn't want to give you any escape clauses earlier. Now that you understand how it is usually in your best interest to wait, I'll tell you when you can disregard that rule.

Recall that the two reasons to wait are that you might be screened out of the interview altogether and the employer might make an offer based on lower previous earnings rather than market value.

Sometimes those two reasons are moot. Creating a new position with an employer is a good example. You won't be screened out, because you'd be the only one interviewing. In a manner of speaking, you've already been offered the job and discussing a market-value range for the position could *help* the employer create that position big enough. Here's an example where discussing money before an "offer" *helped* the negotiations

Cheryl was negotiating with an employer to create an administrative position that included preparing and reviewing large government contracts. Her potential employer could have had a $25,000 administrative assistant position in mind, but she wanted the bottom-line responsibility for making those contracts happen, and she wanted the money that came with that responsibility. She told him that market value for an administrative director of a company their size was in the $45-50,000 range and that she would like him to think along those lines as they assembled the set of responsibilities.

With the correct attitude, "How can we create this position so its value to you is at the administrative-director level?" she worked with him to create responsibilities beyond the clerical. Naming a dollar range helped get her there.

You may find circumstances in which discussing the "dollar size" of the job will help position you better.

So, if salary talk won't screen you out and you think it will help the employer think bigger, you can share your target market value before there's an offer.

But if you just want to tell to avoid tension, think again. Read on.

What if They Get Angry with Me?

People sometimes excuse themselves from following Salary-Making Rule 1 by saying, "If I don't answer the salary question, the interviewer will get angry with me, and then I'll *never* get the job!" Sometimes they're right. Indeed, some interviewers declare a staunch inflexibility about their budgets right away by announcing things like:

- "This position pays X dollars; there's no negotiation. If that's not acceptable to you, then let's end the interview now,"

- "I absolutely have to know your current earnings," or

- "This application must be filled out *completely* before the interview can proceed."

They may feel frustrated that they can't screen you. Sometimes you'll notice that your interviewer seems perturbed, thinks you're not being cooperative. You worry that that will get in the way of building the rapport essential to being hired.

What should you do? Should *you* go first?

First, let me say that inflexibility is the exception. Following the guidelines in Chapters 3 and 4, you will find most interviewers quite amenable to postponing salary talk *once they're assured that you'll accept a fair market-value salary.*

Second, odds are that they're worried you're too expensive. (People rarely get upset about your being too inexpensive.) As long as *you* know that you're interviewing at, or that there's potential to reach, the right level of responsibility, *it's to your advantage* that the company worry about affording you!

A word about tension: Use your common sense to avoid escalating tension to anger. Postponing salary talk is *generally* the best option. But even if you do decide to discuss it up front, remember you can still follow salary-making rules 3, 4, and 5. Poorly executed negotiations are thousands of dollars more valuable than no negotiations at all.

So if you're tempted to go first, to discuss price before value just to placate the interviewer, think twice, then decide.

When you do find yourself in that tension in an interview, remember that, without thinking, your old habits will be in charge and steer you to the path of least resistance: giving in. I'll discuss how *you* can control your habits in the next chapter. For now, if your habits are controlling you, you will feel like going first. If you act on those feelings or on your considered judgment, here are three ways to handle that impulse: least effective (and easiest), better, and best.

Least Effective: The least effective way is to cave in immediately and reveal your salary history or requirements. You risk losing several thousand dollars in that ten-second conversation, and you risk being screened out as too cheap or too expensive. Coughing up a salary figure will get you off the hook, but since it compromises the principles of being hired on value, not price, it's not a tremendously positive sign that you're starting a virtuous cycle.

If, however, you *do* choose the least effective method, at least discuss your salary *expectations* (not your *history*). Determine your market value (see Chapter 5) and communicate a range: "Well, I expect a fair salary for this kind of position. My research indicates a range of X dollars to Y dollars, but every job is unique, so let's discuss the job and my potential in it. Then we'll both have a better idea of my value."

Somewhat better than that: Instead of discussing *your* requirements, discuss the market value, since that's all you want, anyway. Could sound like this, "As I said before, all I need is a fair salary, and here's what my research says the range is, $X to $Y. I think that where I fit in that range will depend on how impressed and confident you are that I can do the job. Can we talk more about that?"

Better still: If you choose to bypass Salary-Making Rule 1 (in which you wait for an offer), there's still a *chance* to follow Salary-Making Rule 2 (in which the interviewer goes first). When the company is adamant about discussing salary, you can probe its budget and say that it's a good starting point. For example: "My salary expectations? They're simple: a fair market value. Perhaps you could help me there; what is the range you're thinking of? I'd be glad to tell you if it fits."

When you get the range, say, "That's in the ball park; I'm sure we can make a good salary agreement if you want to hire me. Let's keep talking."

The Preemptive strike discussed in Chapter 3 is similar to this "let them go first" option. The difference is that instead of turning the tables on the interviewer, you *initiate* salary talk so you're never in the position of answering the question in the first place.

Best: Stick to your principles. You don't have to answer every single question an interviewer asks; you're not on the witness stand. Often you can defuse discomfort by commenting on it, like: "I find talking about money at this point awkward. Perhaps you do, too? I hope I'm not upsetting you by asking to postpone it."

You can finish up with some of the responses at the end of Chapter 4. Nancy's response works well. Or something like: "You see, I know this is the kind of work, and the amount of responsibility, that I want. If I'm valuable to you, I'm sure that finding a fair salary will take care of itself."

This "best" kind of response takes practice. Most people have interviewing habits, and most often they have the specific one of answering every question they're asked, *as if the interviewer really knows what to ask!* I have news for you. Interviewers act out of habit, too! In the final chapter, let's take a look at our habits and their impact on salary negotiations.

Chapter 12
Practice and Coaching

Changing Habits through Practice

This book has supplied the logic, scripts, and tools for strategies that you'll need in order to change your habits about salary talk. But that's not enough. Even if you commit this entire book to memory, when you show up at Mr. Employer's office you'll probably slip back into your same old ways. Unless you practice.

Most of us are not accustomed to negotiating for ourselves. Our present habits push us to do just the opposite: accept what's offered and hope for the best. To understand how to break habits, let's find out how entrenched they tend to be.

Think of all the habits you live out in the first half hour of each day. Turning off the alarm? Pressing the snooze button? Do you find the toothpaste, toothbrush, and hair dryer in the same place every time? If you had to think about each step, and search for the soap and cereal every morning, each would take twice as long *and* not get done as well. For example, you can probably remember the hours it took you to do routine chores when you last moved into a new home and had to establish new habits.

So we must respect habits. They allow us to be comfortable and safe in a rather unpredictable world. On the other hand, old habits can inhibit behavior in a new activity (like salary negotiation) and cost you thousands of dollars.

Let's try an experiment. Put this book down, fold your hands, and notice which pinkie finger is on the bottom. Now, refold your hands with the *other* pinky finger on the bottom. How does it feel?

❑ Comfortable

❑ Uncomfortable

Uncomfortable, naturally!

Which way is correct? Neither, of course. Your way is just your habit; the other way is just the "uncomfortable" way. It makes no practical difference which way you fold your hands, and yet you'll do it the same comfortable way every single time!

A more challenging experiment is to try folding your arms. Notice whether the left arm or the right arm is on top. Go ahead!

Now, try to fold them so that the *other* arm is on top. Difficult, isn't it? Please do it until you can fold them in reverse at will. If you can do it *with ease* in fewer than ten tries, you're terrific. Habits are very strong controllers of even simple behaviors.

Salary and raise negotiations, needless to say, are much more complicated than folding your arms. Poor habits about salary talk will take practice to change. You can practice alone by writing a script, using a tape recorder, or talking to a mirror. An even faster way to change them is through practice *and coaching*.

Practice *and* Coaching Are Even Better

Coaching helps us see ourselves objectively. That's why tennis lessons from a coach will correct in one hour what someone may have tried to correct alone for weeks. The same goes for baseball, football, golf, hockey, aerobics, and jogging. It's true for negotiations, too. Someone with ears *other than your own* can give you objective feedback that will help you handle yourself better. Use friends, counselors, or telephone sessions.

A friend or acquaintance can help you by role playing and asking you the tricky questions. Have your friend read Chapter 3 to understand budget, fudgit, and judgit. That will improve the role playing by helping your friend understand the employer's frame of mind about screening.

Call me; I Love Coaching Salary Negotiations

847-853-1046

Readers have called me many times since this book was first published. I have enjoyed these calls. You, too, are welcome to consult with me and my staff by phone if you wish, at 847-853-1046.

I operate on the "Make You A Buck" principle. Call any time; what we'll do is spend a few minutes to see if my help will really make you money. If so, we'll work at a reasonable hourly rate and coach you what to say, when to say it, and we'll practice.

Here are a few stories to give you a flavor of what we can get done through telecoaching. I've picked some of the more interesting ones because I think you'll enjoy reading them and because you will see a few twists and turns in applying the five salary-making rules in these examples.

Public-Relations Professional

Situation: George called about a salaried public-relations position in a hospital. The hospital was losing money. In the midst of cutbacks and salary freezes, George didn't know how to get a raise. "I'll just be happy to keep my job," he said.

Telecoaching: In reviewing his boss's goals, however, we found that the addictions-treatment center was profitable and the one department on which the boss pinned his hopes for growth.

George and I spotted the boss's hot button, identified a few of George's PR accomplishments especially as they related to the center, and developed the outline of a PR campaign to build the center's visibility and credibility. Although George was not able to get an immediate salary increase, he did negotiate a bonus based on the overall use of the center. We estimated the bonus could net $2,000 to $4,000 a year.

Management Consultant

Situation: A high-level international-business consultant was interviewing for an operations-management position with a nationwide food distributor. The recruiter told Frank that $115,000 was as high as the company would go.

Telecoaching: We were able to find (or find out how to find) three navigation points to guide us: a cost-of-living index, comparable salaries, and a specific trouble spot that Frank could handle with dispatch and save the company $50,000 with. He arranged to negotiate directly with the hiring-decision makers and made his case. Frank got $20,000 more plus a performance bonus of up to 50 percent of his salary.

Village Engineer

Situation: Jim was hired in summer by a small village to be its engineer. He felt the offer was low, but the village manager couldn't go outside the budget, and the budget couldn't be changed until the new village board reviewed it in the fall.

Telecoaching: To get around the problem, however, Jim asked for and got a relocation package (tax free) that was not in the original offer. That boosted his earnings and tided him over until the regular salary-review process could make his earnings more competitive.

Of course, we also set up a plan to make sure the manager *and* the new board would be well informed of his value by the time the fall budget review took place.

Product Manager for High-Tech Marketing Products

Situation: Virginia's stumper was how to negotiate a lateral transfer where she thought (but wasn't sure) she would be making more than her prospective new boss.

Telecoaching: The problem here is that it usually doesn't work well when you talk to a new boss about salary and negotiate for more than the boss is getting. We had to find a way to discover the boss's real salary, then decide how much to negotiate for. We worked out a way to present the dilemma to personnel that allowed the personnel administrator to give Virginia her salary guidelines without actually revealing her boss's earnings. We also strategized a way her new boss might get a raise.

She changed positions, kept her salary, and in the first month taught her boss how to negotiate a better deal for himself as well as for Virginia. Soon they were both earning more than when her negotiations began.

Marketing Manager/Sales Manager

Situation: Dave originally interviewed for a position he was overqualified for. During the interview the sales VP and the operations manager were impressed with Dave, so they called the president in to discuss upgrading the position. They did upgrade it; but just as a camel is called "a horse designed by a committee," the new position was pasted together with two conflicting sets of responsibilities. As it stood, the job was 50-percent sales, sales support, and on-site trouble-shooting, and 50-percent strategic planning. That combination had conflicting elements that would doom it to failure. Dave wanted 10-percent sales and 90-percent planning; he was also pushing for $20,000 more now and even more interesting money later. He also knew that two of the three people in on the decision would fight energetically to keep the job 50-percent sales and sales support.

Telecoaching: First, Dave needed coaching on how to avoid premature salary discussions. Even though his superiors were technically making him an offer, they hadn't really decided for which job. In our discussion it became clear that he was not on Salary-Making Rule 2 (in which the interviewer goes first), but rather on Rule 1, which in Dave's case was: Postpone salary talk until the company knows *which* job it wants to offer.

The strategy we worked out was to concentrate on a five-year plan rather than on a present opening. By submitting a two-page outline of such a plan, Dave was able to pull the attention of all three decision makers to the big picture. He also offered an alternative way to get the 50-percent sales-and-trouble-shooting portion all done without making it half his job. Dave spent a total of twenty minutes delaying and discussing compensation. Finally, he increased the salary $20,000 ($1,000 a minute), and negotiated a profit-sharing bonus based on his five-year performance plan.

Computer Specialist

Situation: Similarly, I told Jerry to break the rules. Usually the base salary is handled first, then the bennies and perks. However, Jerry knew he would want certain pieces of computer hardware to get the results the employer wanted on the job.

Telecoaching: I coached him to say, "Salary and benefits are important, Mr. Employer, but having the tools to do the job for you is my first concern. Let's discuss the important computer investment I want to you to make and, if we can agree on that, I'm sure compensation will be no problem."

While negotiating that perk, Jerry's attitude was: "Even if you offered me a huge salary, I would have to say no if the tools don't come with it." The employer was impressed with his integrity and commitment to results. Jerry got the hardware and a better compensation package to boot.

City Manager

Situation: A city manager had a poor performance review and therefore only a small raise.

Telecoaching: It took us two half-hour sessions to work up a strategy because three of seven city commissioners would change in three months. By rigorous questioning and evaluating, he discovered each commissioner's hot buttons. The manager realized he would need some special management-training and personal-development courses if he was ever going to meet their expectations. By proposing a specific, eighteen-step plan for self-improvement and better performance, he saved his job. (He found out later that the small raise was a first step in a push to get him to quit. The commissioners had actually been planning to terminate him.) He is now well on his way to recouping all his lost-salary ground on his next opportunity.

Direct-Mail Marketer

Situation: Amy had a huge opportunity to make money on the residuals (on the "back end") directly attributable to her work. She was not aware of it and called only to practice her regular negotiation pitch.

Telecoaching: We practiced the regular rules to bring her salary up 10 percent. Then I showed her the back-end gold mine. (See Residual Commission in Chapter 7.) We rehearsed negotiating for bennies on each renewal transaction from original accounts she generated *if and only if* the accounts were profitable from *her* copywriting. Each year thereafter her earnings jumped between $10,000 and $15,000.

On Getting the Courage to Negotiate

The above examples were somewhat complicated; most people's telecoaching needs are much simpler. Often in telecoaching, you'll just confirm and solidify a straightforward application of the five salary-making rules. Sometimes its main benefit is to give needed encouragement and practice.

"I couldn't believe I said what I did." (J. G., clerk.)

"I kept hearing your voice during the interview and I said those magic words....I think I was more surprised at my chutzpah than my boss was.   It helped and it worked."   (T. S., manufacturer's rep.)

"If you hadn't bawled me out for being wimpy, I'd have given up. I'm still a wimp, overall, but at least I'm earning more money!" (L. W., customer-service rep.)

"One needs one's spirit fortified to really stand up for what one deserves. Thanks." (M. C., educator.)

"Hearing you say 'You can do it' made me feel that I could do it....I did it!" (M. B., events planner.)

"He then said, 'Equity?! You want equity too?!' I thought I had gone too far, but I got it, and he was impressed." (B. T., music-company manager.)

"At first I thought, 'This is preposterous! I have no right to ask for all that.'...After [our telecoaching] I saw how I really had been cheating *myself.*   It wasn't my boss's fault, it was me believing that I shouldn't really get...what I deserve. When I finally asked for it, it seemed like the most reasonable thing on earth." (D. W., accountant.)

On Practice

"I kept wanting you to go and talk for me. You had so many great ways to say things. When I finally did it, though, they weren't your words any more. I had used your words enough to make them my own." (K. B., nurse.)

"Practice makes perfect...but for me, practice with you made it possible." (R. D. M., counselor.)

"I thought I knew how to do this. I read the book a hundred times! But it was different saying it out loud somehow. Anyway it worked, thanks." (W. B. C., engineer.)

"Somebody should make everybody rehearse their lines about salary negotiations. Rehearsing answers to every possible response is what made my $5,000 happen." (J. W., salesman.)

"I never could have stated my case like that if we hadn't practiced...I tell my friends that I argued my case with a lawyer and I won!" (M. L., legal secretary.)

Arranging Personal Telecoaching—847-853-1046

If you'd like to strategize, rehearse, or just review what you've been thinking, you are welcome to set up a telecoaching session. Here's what to do. Call me at 847-853-1046 and set an appointment time. My assistant will schedule a time. You can mail or fax me material in advance if you think it would help. At the appointed time, we'll spend a few minutes to make sure this will pay handsomely for you, and if so, we'll have a good go at it. [Sometimes people really have it all handled; in those cases I tell them so and we end it there – no cost.]

If you get the voice mail, rest assured someone will get back to you promptly.

Don't be shy about calling. I love doing telecoachings. Clients report they put a lot of money in the bank from them.

Caution: Don't get into an either-or trap here by either telecoaching with me or practicing with friends. Do both! I encourage you to practice with others in addition to whatever telecoaching you might arrange.

Your Goal in All This

I strongly urge you to practice. Find a friend or coach who will role-play the employer. Have the person probe for your present salary and your expectations, then finally extend an offer to you. You counter with your researched response. Consult Chapters 3 and 4; write out and make up responses that feel right to you. Rehearse them. Tape record a couple of sessions if you wish. *The goal is to make the process comfortable.*

Although negotiating may never be 100-percent comfortable for you, you can still make it sound more and more natural. Many of my clients tell me how, after practicing, their money talk flows smoothly and effortlessly. They *habitually* follow this key principle: value first, price second.

The practice you put in will generate good new habits and a high degree of comfort that the employer will interpret as confidence that you truly deserve what you're asking for.

Final Note: Financial Independence

Increased salaries and raises are nice, but financial independence is even nicer.

I've always been interested in my clients' financial well-being. After witnessing all the career wreckage of corporate downsizing in the '80s, '90s, and post 911, I decided that, besides a better salary right now, I should show clients how to set themselves up for better earnings for their lifetime.

Beginning in 1996, I have made it a point in my counseling work to show clients how to achieve financial independence.

I discovered that you can become free of jobs, salaries, and businesses upon picking one or all of three strategies and applying it consistently in your career. It means attention to working *on* your career, not *in* your career.

Anyone interested in learning about these methods is welcome to request a free email report (with one small condition) called "How to Work Smarter (not Harder) in the Next Seven Years to Cash Out Before It's Too Late" from jkchapman@aol.com.

POSTSCRIPT

Good luck!

I hope reading this book has helped you take your salary more seriously. When compensation is negotiated in a win-win way, both you and your employer will be motivated to get the very best performance and accomplishment from the situation. That, in turn, will produce more money for the employer and career satisfaction and success for you.

May you always be part of the virtuous cycle: achievement ... good pay ... more achievement ... better pay ... even more achievement...

REVIEW OF RESOURCES

Resources for coaching or rehearsing salary negotiations.

Jack Chapman: 847-853-1046, telecoaching service.

Resources for achieving financial independence.

Special report (free with one small condition): "How to Work Smarter (not Harder) in the Next Seven Years to Cash Out Before It's Too Late." Send email request to jkchapman@aol.com.

Resources for salary negotiation presentations.

Salary Negotiation Presentations:

I have several colleagues across the country who speak at bookstores and professional organizations about salary and raise negotiations. If your group might be interested, call 847-853-1046.

Books:

Germann, Richard. Working and Liking It. New York: Fawcett Book Group, 1989. It's old – try Amazon.com

Kravette, Steve. Get a Raise in 60 Days. New York: Bantam, 1983.

Tapes:

Chapman, Jack. How to Beat the System and Get a Raise! (Workshop Tape set and Manual.) Published by the author. (Order directly from Jack Chapman, at 511 Maple Ave., Wilmette, IL, 60091; $69.95 + $3.50 shipping and handling.)

ABOUT THE AUTHOR

Jack Chapman is a nationally known career advisor and speaker in the field of career development. Since 1981, he has personally coached over two thousand individuals in his role as a senior Career Advisor in, and then owner of the Chicago office of the oldest and largest career development firm in the nation.

Now he conducts a private practice named Lucrative Careers, Inc. in which he works with clients two ways: First, to become more satisfied and better paid in their careers, and second, to systematically manage their careers to achieve financial independence. (See "Final Note: Financial Independence" at the end of Chapter 12.)

Through his books, tapes, group work, and training of many other career advisors, he has helped countless people from every walk of life land exactly the jobs, salaries, and raises they've wanted.

He is cofounder and past president of the Professional Career Counselors and Consultants Network (now merged with Association of Career Professionals, International).

Following his undergraduate studies at Loyola University of Chicago, Jack earned his master's in vocational guidance at Northeastern Illinois University and taught on the faculty at Chicago's Columbia College, where he pioneered a career-development curriculum.

Jack has appeared on network television to represent career counselors. He has delivered countless speeches and lectures and conducted numerous workshops and seminars.

Jack welcomes feedback, success stories, and input on this book and the process of salary negotiations, and is available as a speaker and workshop leader for job and career development.

Telecoaching: 847-853-1046 Direct Line: 847-251-4727

Postal Address: 511 Maple Avenue, Wilmette, IL 60091

Web: www.salarynegotiations.com; Email: jkchapman@aol.com